CLARA BOW

MY STORY

"I thought she was the most marvelous star of the 20s because she *was* the 20s, really. Garbo came from Europe, Swanson was already very sophisticated and dressy, and Cecil B. DeMille, but Clara was, as she called herself, the real jazz baby. She got her job in Hollywood, not, as she said very carefully, through a beauty contest. She never thought she was beautiful.
It was a personality contest that she won. Adela Rogers St. Johns did a wonderful series at that time in *Photoplay*, and told about how she grew up. Her father in Brooklyn, on the street. She was absolutely a sensation in the United States in *Dancing Mothers*.
And she was so marvelous. Oh, she just swept the country."

— Louise Brooks

***

"Clara Bow is the quintessence of what the term 'flapper' signifies."

— F. Scott Fitzgerald

Clara Bow

CLARA BOW

MY STORY

As told to Adela Rogers St. Johns
Introduction by A.K. Brackob

HISTRIA
A&E

Histria A&E

Las Vegas ◊ New York ◊ London ◊ Palm Beach

Published in the United States of America by
Histria Books
7181 N. Hualapai Way, Ste. 130-86
Las Vegas, NV 89166 USA
HistriaBooks.com

Histria A&E is an imprint of Histria Books dedicated to outstanding books that focus on arts and entertainment. Titles published under the imprints of Histria Books are distributed in the United States and Canada by Simon & Schuster and worldwide through Unified Book Distribution. We thank readers for supporting authorized editions, which enable publishers to present carefully prepared texts and sustain the work of editors, designers, and scholars.

The original series of articles "Clara Bow – My Life Story" as told to Adela St. Rogers appeared in PHOTOPLAY magazine in the February, March, and April 1928 issues.

Library of Congress Control Number: 2025933041

ISBN 978-1-59211-500-6 (softbound)
ISBN 978-1-59211-620-1 (eBook)

CONTENTS

Clara Bow at 16. The Photo she submitted to a
National Talent Contest that launched her career.

INTRODUCTION

Even the chill of the winter evening in New York City on February 5, 1927, could not deter crowds from gathering in quiet anticipation outside the Paramount Theatre on Times Square. The lights of Broadway reflected off patches of melting snow, and groups of moviegoers, bundled against the winter cold, waited to see the young woman whose rise to fame had captured the national imagination. Clara Bow was returning to the city where she had been born, no longer the anonymous Brooklyn girl she once was, but the young woman whose improbable entry into a studio talent search had opened the door to Hollywood and set her on the path to stardom.

For Clara, the New York City premiere of *It* carried a significance that reached beyond the typical excitement of a major film opening. Los Angeles had given her fame, but New York had shaped her earliest dreams and tested her resilience. This was the city of her childhood—difficult, unstable, and often painful, as she would recount in her memoir—and it was also the place where she first allowed herself to imagine a life in the movies, long before that possibility seemed within reach. Returning now as the lead in the film that would define an era, she stepped out once more into the city she had left, but on entirely different terms.

When Clara emerged from her car, the response from the crowd was warm and immediate. Cheers rose from the sidewalk, and camera flashes flickered. Petite at just over five feet three, and with auburn-red hair and wide brown eyes that audiences instantly recognized, she appeared both glamorous and familiar. The atmosphere felt less orchestrated than a Hollywood premiere, more personal. New Yorkers greeted her not only as a star but as someone who, despite her success, remained connected to the city's neighborhoods and its stories. Clara's smile — open, genuine, and unguarded — reflected that familiarity.

Inside the Paramount, one of the city's most prestigious movie houses, anticipation settled into focused quiet as the lights dimmed. Clara's natural, expressive, and charming performance in *It* quickly drew the audience into the story. Her instinctive acting style, so different from the more theatrical conventions of silent film, resonated immediately. There were moments of laughter, moments of stillness, and the unmistakable sense that something fresh was unfolding onscreen. *Variety* would proclaim, "Clara Bow really does it all, and how."

By the time the curtain closed, a sincere and enthusiastic applause filled the Paramount Theatre. Clara Bow had triumphed not only in Hollywood but now, unmistakably, in her hometown—a homecoming marked by recognition, a moment when New York acknowledged the extraordinary distance she had traveled.

A new archetype had been born, the "It Girl," and its embodiment stood waiting outside on the red-carpeted steps, unaware that her life had just irrevocably changed. That night Clara Bow didn't merely premiere a film; she ignited a cultural phenomenon. Within days, Valentine's Day cards bore her image. Young women bobbed their hair to match hers. Dressmakers copied the slinky gowns she wore. And people lined their walls with her posters. She wasn't simply admired; she was adored. She wasn't simply a movie star; she was a revelation.

Clara's rise to this point remains one of the most remarkable stories in Hollywood history. Born into poverty in Brooklyn, she grew up in a household marked by instability and hardship. Her mother struggled with severe mental illness; her father was unreliable and frequently absent. Clara's childhood was defined by loneliness and fear, punctuated only by the excitement she felt watching the flickering images in neighborhood picture houses. Movies were her escape, her comfort, and the focus of dreams she kept largely to herself.

Her first real opportunity arrived unexpectedly. As a teenager, Clara entered a national acting contest, a studio-sponsored search for new talent. It was a gamble, taken with little expectation of success, but she submitted her photograph and hoped. Against all odds, she won. The prize brought her a screen test and an invitation to Hollywood. It was the turning point of her life: the moment when a girl who had known little but hardship stepped for the first time into the world she had long dreamed of.

Clara's early film work revealed an instinctive talent that distinguished her immediately. At a time when silent film acting relied heavily on exaggerated gestures and carefully rehearsed poses, Clara brought something different — an unaffected naturalism, a spontaneous emotional truth. Her performances radiated an honesty that audiences recognized. Her expressions, often subtle and unstudied, conveyed depths of feeling that required no dialogue. She had a rare gift: the ability to make the screen feel alive.

In the aftermath of the First World War, America was shedding its Victorian skin, embracing jazz, automobiles, speakeasies, and a new kind of woman: independent, modern, unapologetic. By 1927, Clara Bow was not only Hollywood's highest paid actress, but she had become one of the most recognizable faces in American cinema. Her flapper style — bobbed hair, modern fashion, expressive makeup —c aptured the spirit of the Jazz Age. She didn't just play the flapper — she was the flapper. She embodied the exuberance and liberation of the 1920s in a way no actress before or since has matched. Young women imitated her look; young men admired her unreservedly. Yet her appeal went beyond appearance. Clara projected a sense of freedom, individuality, and joy that resonated deeply with a generation eager to break from old constraints.

The premiere of *It* marked the height of this phenomenon. The film's central concept — an intangible, magnetic quality that made someone irresistibly appealing — found its perfect embodiment in Clara. She didn't simply portray a character with "It"; she revealed something audiences recognized before they even had a word for it. Her portrayal of Betty Lou Spence was lively, warm, and effortlessly modern, a reflection of the era she helped define.

Her success continued with *Wings* (1927), the World War I aviation drama that became the first film to win the Academy Award for Best Picture. Though remembered largely for its groundbreaking aerial sequences, *Wings* also benefited from Clara's ability to bring warmth and emotional dimension to the story. In film after film, she demonstrated a consistency and dedication that belied her youth.

But Hollywood of the 1920s was not the glamorous paradise of popular memory. It was an industry built on rigid contracts, relentless production schedules, and punishing publicity expectations. Stars were marketed like commodities, their public images carefully crafted to maximize profit and minimize scandal.

Clara Bow did not fit easily into this machinery. She was too spontaneous, too genuine, too unwilling to hide her feelings. Where other stars cultivated mystery, Clara blazed with transparency. Where others projected refinement, Clara radiated raw vitality. She was real in a world that demanded illusion.

Her frankness extended to her relationships. That candor made her irresistible to audiences but vulnerable to gossip columns that feasted on every fragment of rumor or exaggeration. As time wore on, the pressures of fame, the demands of studio contracts, and the constant attention of the press weighed heavily on her. Stars like Clara were expected to maintain a flawless public image while working grueling schedules and navigating an industry that offered little support for personal struggles.

Behind Clara's vibrant onscreen presence was a young woman carrying the unresolved trauma of her childhood. The vulnerabilities she brought with her often clashed with the expectations placed upon her. Tabloid rumors — some exaggerated, many entirely fabricated — followed her relentlessly. The fast pace of her work and the pressure to produce hit after hit left her with little time for rest, privacy, or healing. Hollywood adored her, but it also consumed her.

In 1928, amid these mounting pressures, Clara made a decision that was both brave and unprecedented for a star of her stature: she chose to tell her story herself. Collaborating with distinguished *PhotoPlay* journalist Adela Rogers St. Johns, she produced a three-part autobiographical memoir titled *My Life Story*.

At a time when Hollywood studios tightly controlled the public narratives surrounding their stars, Clara offered a candid, introspective, and often painful account of her life. Readers were shocked. They had expected glamour; they received a confessional. Clara spoke openly of violence, poverty, betrayal, and emotional scars that had shaped her from childhood. She recounted her mother's breakdowns, her father's neglect, and the loneliness that shadowed her. Yet, her voice emerges with startling clarity — direct, vulnerable, and profoundly human. It is a rare firsthand account from a woman who shaped the very idea of modern celebrity, telling of her struggles with insecurity and her astonishment at the world she suddenly found herself inhabiting. She also tells of the determination that propelled her through circumstances that might have defeated a less resilient spirit.

To understand Clara's place in the broader cultural landscape, it is necessary to consider the era in which she lived. The 1920s, often called the Roaring Twenties or the Jazz Age, were a time of unprecedented change. The world was recovering from the trauma of World War I, and the United States was bursting into an age of prosperity. Automobiles multiplied, radios filled the air with jazz, and cities blossomed with skyscrapers and neon. Social norms were shattered. Young women cut their hair, shortened their skirts, smoked cigarettes, and danced the Charleston until dawn. Prohibition fueled speakeasies, gangsters, and a thrilling undercurrent of rebellion.

Hollywood mirrored and magnified these transformations. The film industry exploded in size and influence. Silent films captivated audiences worldwide, transcending language barriers. The studio system took shape, giving organization to an industry still finding its form. Actors and actresses became icons whose lives were followed as closely as their films.

But before Clara Bow, female stardom followed a simple blueprint: ethereal, delicate, untouchable. Mary Pickford was "America's Sweetheart." Lillian Gish was the fragile, tragic heroine.

Clara changed everything.

She didn't float across the screen; she burst into it. She didn't embody chastity; she embodied life — full, messy, exuberant life. She danced rather than glided. She laughed with her whole body. She flirted without shame. She cried without self-pity. She was not porcelain; she was fire. That fire redefined Hollywood's idea of glamour and reshaped the destiny of the American film heroine.

Clara Bow possessed something that cannot be taught: pure instinct. Unlike classically trained actors, she had no formal education in drama. She didn't need it. Her acting came from the heart, not the stage.

She conveyed emotion with startling clarity using only her eyes and expressions. She could shift from mischievous to heartbroken to incandescent within a single scene. Her body moved with a graceful spontaneity that defied the stiff conventions of silent-era performance.

Clara's naturalistic style was a revelation. While others emoted with grand gestures suited to the stage, Clara's smallest reactions — a raised eyebrow, a turned lip, a sudden sparkle in the eye — connected with audiences on an intimate level. Critics wrote that she made silent film speak.

In this dynamic environment, Clara Bow became not merely a star but an icon. She embodied the era's energy and its contradictions. Her acting — instinctive, expressive, emotionally true — broke from earlier cinematic traditions and anticipated the realism that would define later generations.

Her image as the flapper, the modern woman of the 1920s, captured the imagination of the public and influenced fashion, behavior, and attitudes toward femininity.

Clara's transition from silent films to talkies was smoother than many predicted. While some silent stars struggled with the new technology, Clara's voice — warm, lively, and expressive — connected with audiences. Under the guidance of Dorothy Arzner, one of Hollywood's pioneering female directors, Clara delivered a confident performance in *The Wild Party* (1929), her first sound film. It was a commercial success, affirming her adaptability. Her transition to sound was smooth, but her troubles were only just beginning.

By the early 1930s, exhaustion and emotional strain began to take their toll. The increasing sensationalism of the press intensified the pressures on Clara. The intensifying drive toward moral conservatism in Hollywood, culminating in the formal enforcement of the Hays Code in 1934, made the free expression that embodied Clara's performances increasingly precarious. This hostile climate set the stage for disaster.

The relentless exploitation and press scrutiny reached a critical, destructive peak in 1931 with the sensational trial of her former secretary and confidante, Daisy DeVoe, whom Bow had accused of embezzlement. While DeVoe was eventually convicted, the proceedings immediately devolved from a financial crime into a public dissection of every raw detail of Bow's private life. The courtroom was flooded with false rumors, malicious allegations, and salacious gossip that targeted her finances, her morals, and her mental stability. This highly publicized humiliation was a devastating, final blow, leaving the "It Girl" exposed and battered. Clara Bow realized that Hollywood would not only demand her talent and her fortune but also destroy her peace, making her retreat from the spotlight inevitable.

That same year, Clara found a lifeline in Rex Bell, a Western actor and rancher who offered her a glimpse of a life far removed from the glare of klieg lights and gossip columns. Their courtship was swift, sincere, and welcomed by a public eager for a redemption narrative. Their marriage marked the beginning of a new chapter in Clara's life, far removed from the demands of the film industry. Settling on a ranch in Searchlight, Nevada, she embraced a quieter life as a wife and mother. She devoted herself to raising her two sons, Tony and George, and to the rhythms of rural living. But the emotional challenges she faced were not easily left behind. Clara struggled with mental health issues for many years, reflecting the long shadow of childhood trauma and the pressures of early fame.

Clara Bow passed away from a heart attack on September 27, 1965, at the age of sixty. Although she spent much of her later life away from public view, her influence on cinema and culture endured and, in many ways, has only grown stronger with time. Scholars, filmmakers, and fans continue to revisit her films and her legacy. Her impact on acting, fashion, and the portrayal of modern womanhood remains unmistakable. Recent cultural references, including Taylor Swift's tribute in the song *Clara Bow*, have introduced her to new generations who find inspiration in her authenticity and resilience.

Clara's autobiographical account, published here in book form for the first time since its original appearance in *PhotoPlay* magazine, is one of the most candid documents produced by any Hollywood star of the era. In its pages, she shares the brutality and hardship of her childhood, her mother's breakdowns, and the emotional scars that shadowed her. With astonishing honesty, she recounts her earliest auditions and her battles with depression and anxiety, while simultaneously expressing the joy she found in acting, her astonishment at her own fame, and her gratitude to the audiences who understood her instinctively. It is a document driven by her fears, hopes, and truths, making her voice ring out across a century. To serve as a definitive resource for scholars and fans, this volume concludes with a complete filmography of Clara Bow's cinematic work.

It is impossible to read Clara's autobiography without feeling her sincerity — vivid, breathless, heartbreakingly honest. Her voice rings out a century later with the same immediacy with which she once lit up a movie screen.

Clara Bow's life was a collision of extremes: It was a life defined by abandonment and adoration, poverty and excess, vulnerability and stardom, trauma and triumph. She was America's brightest star in the decade that changed everything. She was the woman who redefined modern femininity. She was the actress whose emotional honesty reshaped cinematic performance. She was the girl from Brooklyn who refused to be broken by the world that tried to defeat her at every turn.

Her story is not simply the story of Hollywood's first "It Girl." It is the story of a woman who rose from unimaginable hardship to become a symbol of freedom, empowerment, and resilience — one whose legend endures a century later. And now, in her own words, she tells that story herself.

In addition to presenting Clara Bow's autobiography in full, this volume also includes a revealing short article she wrote in the early 1930s, near the end of her film career, in which she reflects candidly on motherhood and the shifting direction of her life. To provide readers and scholars with a fuller understanding of her achievements, the book further features a select bibliography and a fully annotated filmography of her complete screen career. Each film entry offers verified production credits, current archival survival status, and an original synopsis highlighting Bow's role, the film's themes, and its significance in the development of her artistry.

A.K. Brackob

CLARA BOW

MY STORY

PART ONE
FEBRUARY, 1928

First Installment of the touching human document of a tragic child who became the very spirit of gayety

***

When I write down at the very beginning that I am twenty-two years old, I can hardly believe it.

I feel much older than that. I feel as though I had lived a long, long time. That is because I have suffered so much, and suffering makes you feel old inside, just as happiness makes you feel young even when your hair is white.

I think this story will surprise you very much. It isn't at all the sort of life story you would expect to belong to Clara Bow. For you know the Clara Bow who has been driven by misery and loneliness to clutch at joy and merriment almost wildly.

There is only one thing you can do when you are very young and not a philosopher, if life has frightened you by its cruelty and made you distrust its most glittering promises. You must make living a sort of gay curtain to throw across the abyss into which you have looked and where lie dread memories.

I think that wildly gay people are usually hiding from something in themselves. They dare not be quiet, for there is no peace nor serenity in their souls. The best life has taught them is to snatch at every moment of fun and excitement, because they feel sure that fate is going to hit them over the head with a club at the first opportunity.

I don't want to feel that way. But I do. When I have told you about my short life, maybe you will understand why, in spite of its incongruity, I am a madcap, the spirit of the jazz age, the premier flapper, as they call me. No one wanted me to be born in the first place.

And when I was born, at first they thought I was dead. They thought every spark of life had been strangled out of me during my long and stormy entrance into this world. They fought for hours, fanning the poor, feeble little flame of life that was in me, and it would flare up and then die down again, quite as though I didn't want to stay.

Everything was against my coming here at all, everything was against my staying here.

There have been a great many times when I wish they hadn't fought quite so hard to keep me here. But I don't feel that way anymore.

I don't know an awful lot about my ancestors or relations. It isn't really strange if my memory is not good, if I am not very definite about facts and dates. I have been trying all my life to forget, not to remember. Besides, young people aren't much interested in family history. At least I wasn't. I don't like my relations, anyway. They never paid any attention to me until I was successful and they weren't kind to me or to my mother when we needed it so much. I try not to have resentment against them, but I don't care anything about them.

My father is the only person I care for, really.

My mother was a very beautiful woman. She came of a good family in New York State and her mother was French and her father was Scotch. They lived on a country place a few hours from New York City. I was never there, because it was gone before I was born. But from what my mother told me it must have been quiet and beautiful and prosperous.

Perhaps that was the reason that my mother didn't want to marry. She idolized her father and loved the home where she had been born and brought up, and that was all she wanted from life. Marriage frightened her. She felt no need of anything more in her life than her father and mother and the quiet life she lead in the country.

On an adjoining farm lived a family named Bow. They had always been neighbors. The Bows were Scotch and English, of the kind I guess that make landed farmers and squires in the old country. There were thirteen children in the Bow family and my mother had always played with them. The youngest of them was a boy, Harry Bow. And he was the darling of the family and just about my mother's age. He was a handsome, talented boy who captivated everybody. He just made people like him so much that they didn't stop to think much else about him. He had a merry laugh, and he could ride and play and was always good-natured and happy.

My mother's mother adored him. When she knew that she was dying, she called my mother to her and told her that this young man had asked for her hand and that she must marry him. My grandmother was very old-fashioned, very French in her thoughts and traditions, and she did not believe that a girl could be happy unless she was married. She said she couldn't die happy unless she knew that her daughter had a husband to care for her and provide for her later years.

They promised.

They were married shortly after she died.

I do not know all the story of what happened here and it is too painful for my father to speak of.

But you see my father had been terribly spoiled. He had neglected his opportunities for education and training. He often speaks sadly now of his wasted youth and I know that is what he means. He had a quick, keen mind, he had imagination, he had all the natural qualifications to make something fine of himself. But he just didn't.

His people thought him too young to marry; they realized he was not able to face the world and take care of himself and a wife. They were very unjust it seems to me, for after all his life had been in their hands. But they cast him off after his marriage.

My mother's people had gradually lost what money they had — they had never been rich -and I think my grandmother must have been the business head of the family, for after her death things went to pieces very quickly, and the home my mother had loved had been sold.

So soon after they were married, my father and mother and her father moved to Brooklyn and my father started a small business there. They lived in a very small place to begin with, only two rooms, and it was hard on them both. My mother had always been accustomed to country life and she always hated the city. My father had never worked and he had always had money and attention. My grandfather was unhappy over the loss of his wife and his home and over being dependent upon them.

I do not think my mother ever loved my father. He knew it. And it made him very unhappy, for he worshipped her always. His devotion to her, his unfailing gentleness and kindness all through the years of her illness is like a miracle to me.

There were two children born before I came along, both girls. One lived two hours. One lived two days.

My mother came forth from the tragedy of that second death a woman broken in health and spirit. I don't think she ever recovered from those two terrible illnesses, nor from the sorrow and horror of losing her two first born babies.

The doctor told her she must never have any more children. And she said over and over that she didn't want any more. They might die, as her two little girls had died. They might leave her without any reward for all she had gone through, without the comfort of a baby's presence which wipes from a woman's mind the suffering of such times.

She didn't want me. Terror possessed her all the time before I was born. Would she die, as the doctor had said? Or, if she survived the ordeal that had nearly cost her her life twice before, would the baby die, as the two others had died? If so, would she lose her reason? She was almost mad with apprehension and fear.

I don't suppose two people ever looked death in the face more clearly than my mother and I the morning I was born. We were both given up, but somehow we struggled back to life.

From that day to the day she died my mother never knew a moment free from ill health of the most shattering kind. She idolized me, but with a strange, bitter love, almost as though she was afraid to love me for fear I, too, would be snatched away from her. She used to watch me when I ran about the house as a little thing, never taking her eyes off me, and in their depths were many things I was too young to read.

I loved her terribly. Her beauty to me was something divine. She had long golden hair that hung way down below her knees, the most beautiful hair I have ever seen. It shone like pure gold. I used to make up fairy stories about it. And her face was pale, almost transparent, with fine, chiseled features.

The pain had worn her face thin, but it hadn't lined it, and still, to me, in spite of all that happened, the word beauty brings up a picture of my mother's white thin face under that mantle of gleaming hair. She was tall and slim and carried herself like a princess, so I think it must be true that she had good blood in her. No woman could have carried herself like that in the midst of so much misfortune unless she had.

When she was mean to me — and she often was, though I know she didn't mean to be and that it was because she couldn't help it — it broke my heart.

I wasn't a pretty child at all, in spite of the fact that both my parents were and such a contrast to each other. My mother so slim and fair, my father a squat strong man, with black hair and twinkling black eyes. My eyes were too black, and my hair was too red.

But I was sturdy and healthy. When I was little people always took me for a boy.

We lived then, and all the rest of the time we stayed in Brooklyn, in the upstairs of a house on a side street in an ordinary neighborhood. I went to the nearest public school and played in the streets like the other children. I always played with the boys. I never had any use for girls and their games. I never had a doll in all my life. But I was a good runner, I could beat most of the boys and I could pitch. When they played baseball in the evening in the streets, I was always chosen first and I pitched. I don't think I had very good clothes, they were rougher and older than the other girls', and the girls used to say snippy things to me and shout "carrot-top" and things like that. Outwardly, it seemed as though I were just a rough, strong little tomboy. But tragedy seemed to mark me early for its own.

I was about five when the first thing that really stands definitely in my mind happened. Clear, with all the little details. All children have those memories, I guess, but oftenest they are happy. Mine are not.

My grandfather, who lived with us, was very dear to me. Father worked so hard and mother was always ill, always strange and depressed, sometimes smothering me with kisses and without a word of any kind for me. My grandfather was the one who played with me and taught me little things and sometimes told me stories. He must have been a very good and gentle old man, for he used to look after mother and me both.

He had built a little swing for me. I used to sit on the floor and watch him while he was making it. He fixed it so that you could pull it up out of the way, on hooks. There wasn't much room, you see. We thought it was a very famous contrivance and perhaps it was. On cold winter days, when I couldn't get out to play, grandfather used to swing me and we had great fun that way.

It was very cold on this particular afternoon. Snow lay everywhere, the whole outdoors was white with it. It was even a little cold in the house. We had always to economize on coal. Sometimes we had to economize on food, too. There was usually enough of these things, but never just plenty, never all you wanted. Scrimping the corners, that's the way it was in our house.

I was cold and lonesome. I went out into the kitchen, looking for something to do. My mother was washing and she didn't speak to me. Her face looked desperately ill, white and weary. I felt she shouldn't be washing. She was washing a red tablecloth for the kitchen table. While I stood there I saw tears dropping from her eyes and splashing into the soapy water. I felt like crying, too.

I went back in to my grandfather and asked him to swing me. He got up and pulled down the swing and began to push me, and pretty soon I forgot I was cold and that mother was crying again, and began to shout with glee. Then, suddenly, the swing gave a violent twist so that I nearly fell out and then it stopped, and I heard a kind of dull fall behind me.

I looked around and my grandfather was lying on the floor. His face was purple and his eyes were open and staring.

My screams brought my mother to the door. In her hands she still held the red tablecloth. It dripped water all over the carpet. She threw it down and ran to my grandfather, saying over and over, "Father, speak to me. Speak to me." She looked so wild I was frightened and ran downstairs and called a neighbor.

They brought a doctor, but it was too late to do anything. He had died instantly, while he was pushing me in my little swing. That was my first encounter with death and I didn't believe it. I was quite sure they were mistaken.

The first night as he lay in his coffin in the dining room, I crept out of my bed and lay down on the floor beside him, because I had a feeling that he might be lonely. My father found me there in the morning, almost frozen. I said, "Hush, you mustn't wake grandfather. He's sleeping." But I knew that he was dead. I missed him very much.

That was a terrible blow to my mother. There had existed a great love and sympathy between them. He was the only one who could make her laugh and talk naturally. Often, when they sat together talking, I would see her pass her hand across her head, as though something cleared away.

After his death, she was sad for a long, long time. She wanted to die, too. She often spoke of it. But she never mentioned suicide. Her courage was too high for that. Though she suffered all the time, more and more, and was depressed, and couldn't seem to rise above it, she went on as best she could.

***

My school life in those earliest days didn't seem to make much impression on me. I have no distinct impression of any of my teachers, or my school mates.

I had one little playmate, though, to whom I was devoted. He was a little boy who lived in the same house with me. I think his name was Johnny. He was several years younger than I was and I used to take him to school with me, and fight the boys if they bothered him. I could lick any boy my size. My right was quite famous. My right arm was developed from pitching so much.

One day after school I was alone in our house upstairs when I heard a terrible noise downstairs. For a minute it curdled my blood, then I ran down wildly. Johnny had gone too near the fire and his clothes had caught and were burning and he was screaming with pain and fright. His mother was standing there, wringing her hands and screaming, too, like a crazy woman, and not doing a thing.

When I came tearing in, Johnny screamed "Clara, Clara, help me." He ran over and jumped into my arms.

I had just enough sense to know what to do. I laid him on the floor and rolled him up in the carpet and tried the best I could to put the fire out. The poor little fellow struggled and screamed all the time.

I shouted for his mother to get a doctor and she ran out. I stayed alone with Johnny, holding him in my arms rolled up in the carpet and trying to soothe him and quiet him. I was crying all the time myself and pretty nearly crazy, too. I seemed to feel the fire on my own flesh, and every time he cried out it seemed to me I couldn't bear it any more.

The doctor came. He couldn't do anything. The little fellow died in my arms. He was just — just all burned up, that's all. I tried to pray then, begging God not to let him suffer like that. The last thing he said was "Clara— Clara—."

When I knew he was dead I went upstairs and cried for hours. I have never cried but once like that since. That was when my mother died. It seemed to me that life was just too terrible to be borne. When my mother came in I was asleep. I had cried myself into complete exhaustion, and I was ill for several weeks. The shock had been too much. For months I used to wake up and think I heard that little fellow calling "Clara— Clara— help me." Things like that are terrible for a little child to go through — I was only about eight or nine, I guess.

As I got older, I played with the boys more and more. I still was an awfully plain kid. I was shy and nervous around girls. They were always hurting my feelings and I thought they were silly anyway. I wore plain clothes and kept my hair tied back out of my face. I was as good at any game as any of the boys. And just as strong. They always accepted me as though I had been one of themselves.

We used to skate together and play baseball and all sorts of rough games in the street and I never felt there was any difference between us. At night, sometimes we would build a bonfire and sit around it after we had skated awhile, and the boys never noticed me. They talked about everything just like they were alone. That was where I learned what boys really think. I knew how they judged girls. I knew which ones they could kiss and how they made fun of them. I was mighty glad they didn't think I was a sissy. I'd do any darn thing to prove I wasn't. We used to hop rides on trucks and get lost and do all sorts of crazy stunts. They let me take care of myself, too, just like I'd been another boy. Once I hopped a ride on behind a big fire engine. I got a lot of credit from the gang for that.

All this time my mother was growing more ill. She had always been subject to fainting spells and they grew gradually worse. They weren't fits and they weren't regular fainting spells. Often they would happen two or three times a day, and then maybe she would be free from them for a long time. When she felt them coming on she would look at me so pathetically. Like a woman caught in some trap. Then her eyes would grow glassy and she would start to gasp for breath. It was just as though she were being strangled. She would fight and fight for breath.

Usually I was alone with her, and I would run to her and massage her throat to try to make her breathing easier. I'd say, "Mother, mother, don't — please don't." When father was there sometimes we'd cry together, because it is terrible to see someone you love suffer like that and not be able to help them.

We never had much money, you know, and so we couldn't consult any specialists. Our own doctor told us it was a nervous disease. My father said her mother had once told him that when she was a child she had a bad fall on her head. When I was four years old she fell again, on the stairs, and it opened up the old scar. They had to take stitches in it. Probably advanced brain specialists today would tell us that that had a lot to do with it. Perhaps they might have helped her, but we didn't know what to do.

Of course when she was having her bad times I had to do most of the house work and the washing and cooking. Father had had a lot of bad luck. Everything seemed to break against him. He worked as a carpenter or an electrician, or at any odd jobs that he could get to do. Everything seemed to go wrong for him, poor darling. He wanted so much to do more for us and he worked so hard, but just bad luck followed him all the time. So I had to do the best I could taking care of mother and the house, but I wasn't very good at it. I never had any knack about housework, or cooking. I got to be a pretty expert nurse for mother, but it always frightened me when she got bad and I dreaded seeing her suffer.

When I first started to the Bayside High School in Brooklyn, I was still a tomboy. I wore sweaters and old skirts made over from my mother's. I didn't give a darn about clothes or looks. I only wanted to play with the boys.

I guess I was about fourteen or maybe fifteen when my mother had quite a long spell of being almost herself. Her health was better and things brightened up quite a good deal. Then she began to take a little interest in my clothes and my looks. She combed my hair a new way, so the curls fell around my face, and she made me a pretty dress, that was cut in at the waist and showed pretty plainly that I wasn't a boy after all.

Right away there was a change in the boys' attitude toward me. Oh, I was heart-broken. I couldn't understand it. I didn't want to be treated like a girl.

There was one boy who had always been my pal. We always fought each other's battles and he used to catch on the baseball team I pitched for. Well, one night when we'd been out skating, he kissed me on the way home.

I wasn't sore. I didn't get indignant. I was horrified and hurt. It seemed to me that the end of everything had come. I knew now that I could never go back to being a tomboy. The boys wouldn't let me. They'd always liked me so well, I'd always been their favorite. Not to kiss or be sweet on, but because I was game and could run fast and take care of myself. They'd always liked me better than those sissy girls that put powder on their noses.

Now that was over. No matter how much I wanted to be a tomboy still, I couldn't. The boys wouldn't let me.

I wasn't ready for the dawning of womanhood, for the things that would take place of what I had lost. I'd been cast out by my pals. The girls still made fun of me for being a tomboy. I was absolutely alone.

I had never liked to study. I was just skimming along because I was naturally quick, but I never opened a book and the teachers were always down on me. I don't blame them. I guess I must have looked pretty hopeless. But I often think now, when I come of myself to realize how I love reading, how much I want to know things, that it wasn't all my fault. If they had made me see what I see now, by myself, I know I would have been good.

In this lonesome time, when I wasn't much of anything and hadn't anybody except Dad, who was away most of the time, I had one haven of refuge. Just one place where I could go and forget the misery and gloom of home, the loneliness and heartache of school.

That was to the motion pictures. I can never repay them what they gave me.

I'd save and save and beg Dad for a little money, and every cent of it went into the box office of a motion picture theater. For the first time in my life, I knew there was beauty in the world. For the first time, I saw distant lands, serene, lovely homes, romance, nobility, glamour.

My whole heart was afire, and my love was the motion picture. Not just the people of the screen, but everything that magic silversheet could represent to a lonely, starved, unhappy child. Wally Reid was my first sweetheart, though I never saw him except on the screen. He was Sir Galahad in all his glory. I worshipped Mary Pickford. How kind and gentle and loving she was. Maybe there were people like that in the world.

A great ambition began to unfold in me. I kept it hidden for fear of being laughed at. I felt myself how ridiculous it was. Why, I wasn't even pretty. I was a square, awkward, funny-faced kid. But all the same I knew I wanted to be a motion picture actress. And I can say one thing, right here. If I have had success beyond my own greatest dreams, it may be that it is the reward for the purity of my motive when I first dreamed that dream. For I truly didn't think of fame or money or anything like that. I just thought of how beautiful it all was and how wonderful it must be to do for people what pictures were doing.

One day I saw in a paper an announcement of a contest. Not a beauty contest. I wouldn't have dared to enter that. This said that acting ability, personality, grace, and beauty would be judged in equal parts.

I went to Dad. Shyly, I told him my dream. He was so kind. He always understood. He was harassed and miserable and overworked, but he was kind and understanding always.

He gave me a dollar. I knew, even then, what a sacrifice it was to him. I went down to a little cheap photographer in Brooklyn and he took two pictures of me for that dollar. They were terrible.

Without daring to tell mother, I sent them in to the contest. And sat down to wait and pray.

***

No star ever has spoken so frankly, so bravely about her childhood and early struggles. No actress has written more dramatically or truthfully about her rise to fame. In the second installment of her Life Story, Clara Bow tells Adela Rogers St. Johns about her first pathetic efforts to find a place for herself in the movies. You won't want to miss a word of this great Life Story.

IT '5487
CAL 29

Clara in *Call Her Savage* (1932)

PART TWO
MARCH, 1928

Miss Bow tells of the days when ridicule, disaster and defeat nearly ended her career.

Last month Clara Bow told how her mother, who was of French descent, married her father, the youngest of a neighboring Scotch-English family of fourteen. The newly married couple moved to a small place in Brooklyn. Clara's father had difficulty making a place for himself. Troubled days came. Their first two children died almost at birth. Clara was the third. She grew up to be the tomboy of the neighborhood. She never had a doll in her life — but she had a place on the street corner baseball team.

At school Clara read of a motion picture contest. She went to a photographer and had two pictures made for a dollar. They were terrible, but she sent them to the contest judges

***

Hope is a funny and wonderful thing. Every bit of reason I had, every logical thought process I followed, told me I had no chance to win any contest to enter motion pictures. It was silly to even dream of it. There wasn't a single person who knew me, except my Dad, who wouldn't have laughed long and loud at the mere idea. Why, the contest was open to everyone in the United States. The world was full of beautiful girls, girls with clothes and education and advantages of every kind, who wanted to go into pictures. They would enter such a contest.

What chance would I have?

I lay awake night after night telling myself all these things, preparing myself for what I felt was an inevitable disappointment.

Yet hope went on singing in my breast. Sometimes I think that is why hope was included with faith and charity by St. Paul, as the greatest thing to possess. Hope is the thing that enables us to try to accomplish the impossible, that urges us on to heights that, without the encouragement of its music, we would never dare attempt.

Finally, a letter came. My hands were cold as I opened it. I don't think I breathed for several minutes. I was afraid to look. At last I did. It told me to come to the magazine offices.

That didn't mean anything. The judges in this contest were Howard Chandler Christy, Harrison Fisher and Neysa McMein. Judges of beauty, all right. No fooling them. Still, it was one tiny step nearer.

My school work was going all to pieces under the strain. I couldn't keep my mind on it for a second. I was just one big pulse of hope and excitement. Every teacher I had — I was in my third year — was sour at me. But I couldn't help it.

On the day set, I went to the contest offices. I sat rigid all the way. It seemed that ages passed. I had a fantastic idea that my hair would have turned from red to white by the time I arrived.

The office was full of girls and my heart just flopped when I saw them. Every bit of hope and assurance oozed right out through my boots. Oh, they were pretty girls. To me, they seemed the most beautiful girls in all the world. Blondes and brunettes, no vulgar little redheads. They were elegantly dressed, perfectly groomed, with lovely manicured hands and slim, delicate legs in sheer stockings. They had poise.

I hadn't dressed up because I had nothing to dress up in. I had never had a manicure nor a pair of chiffon stockings in my life. I had never even been close to the scent of such perfumes as filled that room. I wore the one and only thing I owned. A little plain wool dress, a sweater and a woolly red tam. I hadn't thought much of that angle. I had only looked at my face, and that was disappointment enough.

But now, in this gathering, I was painfully aware of how I was dressed. I felt presumptuous to be there at all. Shame and humiliation overcame me.

Those girls didn't leave me much room for doubt that the impression I made was as bad as I thought it would be. Eyebrows went up, noses elevated, there were snickers here and there. At first I wilted. Tears came up and choked me, but I beat them back somehow. I had learned not to cry in a hard school — on the pavement of Brooklyn with a gang of boys.

But slowly rage began to well up in me. Why should they look at me like that? Why need they be so unkind? I wasn't much, but I knew I wouldn't be as cruel as that to anyone that was worse off than I was. Suffering had taught me how bitter suffering can be, and I never, never wanted to inflict it on anybody else.

So I managed to keep my chin up and my eyes began to blaze and for a moment I reverted back to the little street tomboy and wanted to sail into those pretty, painted, perfumed girls.

Just then the door opened and some men and a couple of ladies came out. They walked around the room, looking everybody over, very carefully, as though they had been so many statues. I tried to keep out of sight, I didn't know who the people were and I was too busy trying to keep from crying to have an idea of posing or making an impression.

Suddenly one of the men said, "There's an interesting face — that kid with the red tam and the gorgeous eyes."

I looked around. I was the only girl with a red tam. The blood came singing up and nearly suffocated me. The words kept ringing in my ears. "Interesting face." "Gorgeous eyes." Me— Me— little Clara Bow.

They went back in. Several girls went in, came out. Pretty soon, I was called. A few minutes before I thought of how I'd ritz those girls, if I should happen to get a summons. But when they called me I was too excited to remember a detail like that. They talked to me. What made me think I could act?

Well, I couldn't exactly tell them. I don't know why I can act — if I can. Only, in the many hours I had spent in motion picture theaters I had always watched intently and I had always had a queer feeling about actors and actresses on the screen. Sometimes what they did seemed just right. Again, I felt they were doing it wrong. I knew I would have done it differently. I couldn't analyze it, but I could always feel it. It just threw me right out of the feeling of reality about a picture when an actress made a gesture or used an expression that seemed wrong to me.

I tried to explain, and they all laughed a little, but kindly. And said I should wait for a test.

I think there were about twelve girls who had made tests that day.

They all wanted to do it first. I didn't. So I never said a word. I sat there, though, through every one of those tests and watched everything that was done, everything they were told, every mistake they made. They all had to do the same thing — walk in, pick up a telephone, laugh, look worried, then terrified. I got it finally so I knew how I was going to do it and just what I was going to think about while I was doing it.

Gradually, little by little, the tests narrowed down. I went back and forth, making new ones as more and more were eliminated. Each time I expected to be the next one to go — but I didn't. It was tough getting the carfare and I had only the one dress.

I had been out of school a lot, going over to New York, and the teachers had been complaining and telling me I was sure to flunk. What did it matter? If I failed in this, I'd go to work somewhere.

The day I went to the offices — it had in some marvelous fashion narrowed down to a statuesque blonde beauty and me — I got home about five o'clock.

Mother was sitting motionless in the dining room. Her face was white and I had never seen her eyes look like that, even when she had her worst spells.

She said, "Where have you been?"

Just that in the most awful, cold tone.

It seems that one of the teachers from high school had been there to tell her how much I was absent and that I would fail if something wasn't done about it.

Well, I told her where I had been and what I was doing. I told her it looked as though I had a chance to win this contest and if I did it meant a job in the pictures and a chance to make good and I could do a lot of things for her.

She fainted dead away, not one of her choking fits, but just a dead faint. I was so scared I hardly knew what to do. I ran and tried to lift her up and threw water on her. She didn't come to for a long time and when she did she just cried and cried.

"You are going straight to hell," she said. "I would rather see you dead."

I had never dreamed she would feel like that. I hadn't told her because I didn't want to disappoint her and put her through the strain of waiting, she was so nervous. Besides, I was ashamed. I knew she didn't think I was pretty or clever, and I thought she'd say I was a fool.

Dad came in just then and we tried to soothe her, but she just sat and stared at me, with those awful, burning eyes, and her face was so white and still.

So I cried, too, and promised her I'd give it up right away.

But Dad told her she had no right to ask such a promise of me. He said he knew I had talent. He said I might not be pretty, but I was different, I was a type. He said I had a chance for a real success, with a big future and that outside that the best I could hope for was a job in a store or an office with long, hard hours, and little pay and no future. He said pictures weren't any more dangerous for a girl, they weren't as dangerous as working in stores and offices and that I had always been a good girl and she had no right to feel that way about me.

For a long time she didn't answer, just sitting there white and still, her hands hanging down. At last she said, "All right."

Three days later they sent for me and told me I had won the contest and would have a good part in a picture and all the publicity that had been promised and everything.

It was hard for me to believe. I kept thinking they'd change their minds and every time the postman stopped at our door my heart stopped beating. They told me the judges had picked me because I was "different" and had a unique personality.

I went back to high school and told them. The girls only laughed at me. Oh, how they laughed. They just decided that any beauty contest I could win must be a bum one. Every time they looked at me they giggled and giggled. So I decided not to go to school any more. It hurt to be laughed at. I thought maybe they would be glad.

Then began a terribly hard time. I guess all contests are like that. For weeks, nothing happened. I waited and waited. I haunted the office. Panic was growing inside of me, driving me crazy. After all I had been through, all my great joy, was this going to be a failure?

But at last I hung around so much they decided to get me a job to get rid of me. Or maybe they really meant to all the time and were just busy. Christy Cabanne was making a picture with Billy Dove as the star. They took me over to him and explained the situation and he took one look at me and almost had a fit.

"Don't tell me she won a beauty contest," he said.

It almost broke my heart.

Anyway, he agreed to give me a small part.

But there was another stumbling block. I had to have four dresses to play the part and I had to furnish them myself. I didn't have four dresses. I didn't have one dress. Dad didn't have any money — yes, he had enough to buy about half a dress. So then I did something I'd never done before. I put my pride in my pocket and for the first and last and only time I went to some of my relatives for help.

I had an aunt in New York who was rich. They had a beautiful home and one of the girls had made a good marriage and the son was in Wall Street or something. I had never been in their house, but I went. I told my aunt the whole story. I didn't need much and I would pay it back out of the first salary I got. It was my big chance and it looked like I was going to lose it because I didn't have four dresses.

She put me out of the house.

While I was walking away, just sunk, I heard footsteps behind me and somebody called my name. It was her son, my cousin. He didn't know me at all, but he had heard our conversation. He was interested in pictures, and he didn't think about them as his mother did.

"I don't think you've got a chance, kid," he said, but I like your spirit. Here's all the change I've got."

He handed me eighty dollars.

Eighty dollars may not sound much to buy four dresses. It wasn't. But it was so much more than nothing. I went to a second hand place, to a wholesale place, and I got four dresses. I know now they must have been pretty terrible. But then I thought they were magnificent.

The next day I went to the studio ready to work.

I had never put on a make-up. While I was doing the tests for the contest they had an actress who made up all the girls. Now I had to go alone. But I was encouraged when they put me in a dressing room with four other girls. I thought surely they would help me. But they didn't. They just laughed. They said, "Go ahead and learn like the rest of us did."

Sometimes I wonder about things like that. Most of the people in pictures are so kind. It seemed as though fate were just throwing everything in my way, giving me every possible obstacle. I don't think those girls meant to be unkind. They were careless and self-centered. Most of the unkindness in the world comes from thoughtlessness. I am sure of that.

I did the best I could. When I came on the set, Mr. Cabanne thought I had gone crazy. I looked like a clown. I tell you I didn't have to use any cold cream to take that grease paint off. I washed it off with good hot tears. The next day I watched the other girls and learned a little and got by all right.

My part wasn't very big but I had about five scenes. In one of them I was suppose to cry. Mr. Cabanne didn't seem to think I could, but I did. It was always easy for me to cry. All I had to do was think of home. He said I had done it well and it seemed to please him. After that, he was kinder, and helped me.

***

When the picture came to Brooklyn I was so excited I couldn't sleep. I asked some of the girls from school to go with me to see it. I guess maybe I wanted to show off a little. I wanted to prove to them what I could do. I thought of those five scenes and I felt sure they'd respect me after that. I'd be a real movie actress.

We went. They ran the picture. There wasn't a single shot of me in it anywhere.

The girls certainly made life miserable for me. You can't blame them. But it was a bitter blow to me.

But not the worst one.

Mother was growing steadily worse and her thoughts seemed to center on me.

She came up to me one day on the back porch where I was doing some washing and she said, "I think I'll kill you. You would be much better off dead. This is a terrible world. Motion pictures are terrible. I think it is my duty to kill you."

I was frightened but — it was more than that. I was so sorry for her, I loved her so. I knew she loved me. I never mentioned pictures to her after that, but every once in a while she would start talking about how it was her duty to kill me. I told Dad and it worried him terribly and we had a new doctor but he said there was nothing he could do.

Things weren't breaking for me at all. Winning the contest hadn't seemed to mean a thing. I wore myself out trying to find work, going from studio to studio, from agency to agency, applying for every possible part. But there was always something. I was too young, or too little, or too fat. Usually, I was too fat. When I told them that I'd won this contest, they only laughed. They said the woods were full of girls who'd won some bum beauty contest and they were mostly dumb or they wouldn't have been in any beauty contest in the first place. Which I guess maybe was right. And I couldn't wear clothes and I wasn't pretty enough.

But finally I got a job. Elmer Clifton was going to make a picture called Down to the Sea in Ships. He wanted a small, tomboy type of girl to play a second lead. He hadn't much money to spend and he couldn't afford to pay much salary for this part. He had been at a casting agent's office and they had been going over all the people they knew without hitting the right one. The contest manager had sent Mr. Clifton copies of the magazines containing my picture. After the agency visit he happened to open one of them to a picture of me. It was one in the red tam and was part of the publicity from the contest, so you see it did do me some good.

He said, "Who the dickens is that? Clara Bow. Cute name. That's what I want. Send for that kid."

They sent for me.

But I was terribly discouraged by then. I was so sick of being told I was too young or too small. So I decided to take a desperate chance. I put my hair up, sneaked one of mother's dresses and went over done up like that.

When Mr. Clifton saw me he said, "Great heavens, you're not the girl I saw in the picture. I wanted a kid, to play a tomboy part. You won't do at all."

Just think. I had guessed wrong and nearly missed my chance. I started explaining so fast the words stumbled over each other. I said, "Oh, I'm the girl all right. But I've lost so many parts because I was too young that I put on mother's clothes to see if I couldn't look older."

That made him laugh and I went home and got my own clothes and came back and got the part at fifty dollars a week. That was more money than I knew there was in the world.

But we had to go away. They were going to make the picture up in New Bedford. I'd never been away from home a night in my life and I knew mother wouldn't let me go. But Mr. Clifton arranged for the cameraman's wife to go along and be with me as a chaperon — so Clara Bow went on her first location with a chaperon.

***

I went home all happy and thrilled. Mother was sitting there, and she was very quiet and didn't say much. She looked well, though, there was color in her face. Father was working and we had dinner and she was quiet, but very pleasant and sweet. Then I went to bed. I hadn't told her about the job. I thought I'd wait until father was there. I don't know how long I had been asleep when I woke up and realized there was somebody in the room. My heart was beating hard and funny. The door was a little open and in the light from the other room I saw mother standing there, in a white nightgown. Her hair was braided over each shoulder and hung down to her knees. In her hand was the butcher knife.

I said, "Mother?"

She didn't answer. Just came closer to the bed.

I said "Mother, darling, what are you doing?"

She pinioned my hands down. "I'm going to kill you, Clara." She said very quietly. "It will be better."

She put the knife at my throat.

The room went all black. I fought to keep consciousness. I knew if I didn't I was lost — we were both lost. I kept thinking. "Oh, poor mother, poor mother, how terrible she will feel if she ever knows she has done this. I mustn't let her."

I moved. The knife came closer. The hands tightened like steel.

I started to talk, to plead, to soothe, watching her all the time. She didn't seem to hear me. Her eyes burned into mine. I don't know how long it was, but it seemed hours. At last, when she seemed to relax for a final effort, I made a desperate spring, as swiftly, as strongly as I could. It knocked her away from me. I ran across the room and out the door and turned and locked her in.

Outside I was so weak I could hardly move. I could hear her inside trying the door. The handle turned. I wanted to go back in and comfort her. But I was afraid to. It was too terrible to stay alone. I went downstairs and asked the lady there if I could sit there awhile. She looked at me, but didn't ask me any questions and she said I could stay.

I sat there all night. At five o'clock, I heard Daddy's step. I ran to meet him. Poor Daddy. We went up together. There was no sound from the room. We opened the door and se was sleeping on my bed, as peacefully as a child, her hands folded, the long, golden braids over her shoulders. When she woke up she didn't know anything about it.

I was glad to go away then. She didn't make any objection, when Dad explained it to her. But the shock had upset me more than I knew. All the thirteen weeks we were on location I was ill. I knew it was only nerves and I fought against it. But I couldn't sleep. I used to wake up crying all the time.

When I came home, mother was there. Dad told me he had had her away in a sanitarium for treatment. They said she wasn't insane. You couldn't call her that because she was so intelligent. She could answer any question, talk well, be as calm.... Then once in a while these spells came on. But she seemed so much better Dad brought her home. She wanted to be at home. But she began to be unhappy again about my going into pictures. Once she said, "You don't take me to the studio with you. You're ashamed of me. You think I'm crazy." That broke my heart. I was so proud of her.

So I decided to give up pictures. Maybe mother would be better. I couldn't bear to make her unhappy like that. So I hunted around and got a job answering the phones in a doctor's office. I hated it. The trip was long and the pay small, but it was all right.

And then, I started trying to have a little fun. I just had to. I knew a lot of young people around Brooklyn, boys I'd been to school with. They were always asking me to go places. The boys seemed to like me and I liked them, though I had never been in love, not even a kid romance. I never had a love affair until after I went to Hollywood.

One night I went to a party with some young friends, two boys and a girl. We were having a fine time, dancing and playing the phonograph, just like a bunch of kids will, when the telephone rang.

It was my father, and he said I was to come home right away.

I didn't want to go. I said: "Oh, Dad, please don't make me. I'm having such a good time. If mother's having one of her spells, she'll come out of it all right."

That was the only time I'd ever said anything like that. But I was only a kid and I wanted a little fun.

But Dad insisted. He said, "You'd better come right away, Clara."

PART THREE
APRIL, 1928

In this final installment Miss Bow tells about her first success, her loves and her philosophy of living.

In the previous installments of this engrossing story, Clara Bow told of her early life in Brooklyn; of her love for her father; of her devotion to her pathetic mother. Clara was the tomboy of the neighborhood — a strange, vivid but far from pretty child.

She entered a motion picture contest and won a prize. But when she tried to find work in the studios, she was snubbed and ignored. Her mother, desperately ill, fought against Clara's career. One night, in a fit of insanity, she tried to kill Clara. After getting her first chance in Down to the Sea in Ships, Clara decided to give up pictures, for her, mother's sake. Then, one night, she is called home from a party by an urgent message from her father.

***

That night, after my father called me on the telephone at the party and told me to come home, we went through the dark streets in silence. All the laughter and gaiety had fled. We were just scared kids. I remember thinking then that fun didn't seem to last very long, that something terrible always happened, and maybe it was best to get all you could out of it when you could.

Mother was on a couch in the living room. She was white and still. She did not know me. She never knew me again, though I used to try so hard to make her. For days, she lay like that and I cared for her, trying to ease the paroxysms of pain when they came.

And just then, with the particular way fate has of always bringing extremes into my life, my first chance in pictures came. They sent for me to play a little dancing girl in *Enemies of Women*. At first, I didn't want to do it. I didn't think I could, my heart was so heavy. But there was nothing I could do for mother and Dad insisted that I go ahead. He saw that I was breaking down under those days of silent grief, of being shut up all the time in one room with mother like she was.

It was only a bit in the picture. I danced on a table. All the time I had to be laughing, romping wildly, displaying nothing for the camera but pleasure and the joy of life. As I say, it was only a bit, but no matter what parts I have been called upon to play as a star, or ever will be, not one of them could compare in difficulty to that role. I'd go home at night and help take care of mother; I'd cry my eyes out when I left her in the morning — and then go and dance on a table. I think I used to be half-hysterical, but the director thought it was wonderful.

One day when I was on the set working, in some sort of a little scanty costume, I looked up and saw father standing there. One look at his face told me that the end had come. I walked over to him and just stood staring. I was paralyzed. I don't think I had realized until that moment that mother was really going to die. And I don't think I had ever realized how much I loved her.

Looking back on it now, it seems to me that the day of my mother's funeral was the beginning of a new life for me. Perhaps it was the birthday of the Clara Bow that you know. The end of my kid life had come. Sorrow and disappointment had been my lot so much that I didn't believe in anything but trying to get what you could out of life. I've come to a saner philosophy now, But then I was just hard and bitter.

On that day, we went across to Staten Island on the ferry, and I sat absolutely motionless all the way, my hand cold and frozen in my dad's. All feeling had left me. Loneliness engulfed me. Even during the services, in the church and at the grave, I didn't cry. Dad said my face was like a piece of marble. Poor dear, he was weeping enough for two of us, but I couldn't cry. When they started to lower the coffin into the ground, my heart began to beat again. Then the clergyman turned and told me to throw the first pieces of earth down upon her I had so greatly loved.

At that, I came to life and went crazy. I tried to jump into the open grave after her. I screamed and cried out that they were all hypocrites, they hadn't loved her when she was alive, or cared for her, or done anything to make life easier. I raved and fought like a little wildcat. The thought of leaving her there in that hard, cold ground tortured my imagination beyond bearing.

And then I was overcome with remorse. Just think, when she felt the way she did about pictures, I'd actually been working, dancing on a table with just a few clothes on, when she left me for good. A deep knowledge, perhaps the deepest emotion I had ever had in my life, came to me then of how much she had loved me. I'd been the only thing she'd ever had to love, she'd poured all the frustration of her soul out upon me. And I'd disappointed her, gone against her wishes.

I felt that I never wanted to see another motion picture. I was very ill again after that. And for a while I stuck to my resolution about motion pictures. But Dad — who is so very sensible, who knows the world well and understands so much — talked it all over with me. I remember he came in and sat on the end of my bed one night and looked down at me.

"Little daughter," he said, "you're making a big mistake. You're very young and I know you think your heart is broken. But it isn't. You mustn't allow it to be. You have a long life ahead of you, and your mother

— as she was before her illness changed her — would want you to go on and live it to the fullest. She was a very wonderful woman and she expected a great deal of you. It would make her so unhappy to know that your grief is ruining your life. And at the time when she was herself, she would have understood your ambition, your desire to be in pictures. She loved beauty and all expressions of it. So you must, for her sake and your own and mine — because after all, Clara darling, I'm still here and I need you, too — you must pull yourself together and do your work."

That woke me up. I hate a quitter and I saw that I was quitting. And I knew he was right, that if mother had been herself she would have understood my picture work. So I started in again looking for work. I don't believe anybody had a harder time getting started in pictures than I did.

You see, I had to make a niche for myself. If I am different, if I'm the "super-flapper" and "jazz-baby" of pictures, it's because I had to create a character for myself. Otherwise, I'd probably not be in pictures at all. They certainly didn't want me.

I was the wrong type to play ingenues. I was too small for a leading woman and too kiddish for heavies. I had too much of what my wonderful friend Elinor Glyn calls "It," apparently, for the average second role or anything of that sort. I got turned down for more jobs, I guess, than any other girl who ever tried to break into pictures.

Finally I did get a lead with Glenn Hunter. The girl was a little roughneck, and somehow they thought I fitted into it. I guess I did. I'd always been a tomboy, and at heart I still was. I worked in a few pictures around New York and by that time *Down to the Sea in Ships*, which had been held up for such a long time, was released and that helped me.

About this time, I met a woman in New York who was sort of a casting agent. I am not going to mention her name in this story because I am trying to be truthful all the way through and I cannot say anything kind about her. Perhaps she did try to help me, but she did so many things that didn't help and while I try not to hold any hard feelings against anyone, I cannot help feeling unhappy whenever I think of her.

Anyway, about that time Mr. Bachmann saw me in *Down to the Sea in Ships*, and he liked my work. He came to talk to me. At that time, he was B.P. Shulberg's partner and he wired Mr. Shulberg, who was in Hollywood, that he thought I was a "bet." He suggested that Mr. Shulberg give me a three months' contract and my fare to Hollywood, at a salary of fifty dollars a week, and give me a chance.

"It can't do any harm," he said.

So this agent — I'll call her Mrs. Smith, because that wasn't her name — and I came to Hollywood.

We left my Dad in New York, because we didn't have the money for railroad fares and besides he'd gotten a job down at Coney Island, managing a little restaurant, and he liked it. So we thought we would wait and see how I made out.

Mrs. Smith and I took a little apartment in Hollywood and I started to work. I did nothing but work. I worked in two and even three pictures at once. I played all sorts of parts in all sorts of pictures. In a very short time, I had acquired the experience that it often takes years and years to get. It was very hard at the time and I used to be worn out and cry myself to sleep from sheer fatigue after eighteen hours a day on different sets, but now I am glad of it.

The story of my career from there on isn't so different from the story of all other motion picture careers. I'll wind it up later, but right here I'd like to stop and tell you something of my personal life in Hollywood and the three love affairs — or engagements — that have happened to me since I came and that have been so much in the newspapers.

You know enough about me to realize that I'd never "had things." I'm not going to pretend that I had. Everything was new and wonderful to me. It was wonderful to have the things I wanted to eat, not to have to scrimp on dessert, and be able to order the best cuts of meat. It was wonderful to have silk stockings, and not cry if they happened to get a run in them. It was wonderful to have a few dollars to spend, just as I liked, without having to worry about the fact that they ought to be used to pay the gas bill.

Maybe other people don't realize that, don't get the kick out of those things that I do. Of course, I still can't exactly understand the money that is coming and is going to make my Dad and me comfortable and happy all the rest of our lives. When I bought my first home, the one I still live in, a little bungalow in Beverly Hills, when I signed the check, I couldn't possibly appreciate what the figures meant. I knew I had that much in the bank — me, little Clara Bow — and that the home was mine and I'd actually earned it. But the figures were just too big for my comprehension.

But I do know what a hundred dollars is. That used to be a dream to me — to have a hundred dollars. I never thought I would, not all at once — have a hundred dollars, and certainly not to do something I really wanted to do with. So now I get more thrill out of a hundred dollars that I can go and buy a present for a friend with, or do something for Dad, or get myself something awfully feminine and pretty with, than I do out of my salary check.

I guess I'm still just Clara Bow at heart.

I'm getting away from the run of my story, but a life story ought to tell you a little about how a person feels, and that's how I feel about the success that has come to me.

Well, a short time after I'd come to Hollywood and Mrs. Smith and I were living in a little apartment, and I was working in three pictures at once, I met Gilbert Roland.

I'd never been in love all my life. Funny, because I suppose people think I was born being in love with somebody. But Gilbert was the first man I ever cared about. There isn't any reason why I shouldn't tell it, because we were both kids, and we were engaged, and we were very happy. Not a bit in the modern, flapper fashion, but rather like two youngsters that didn't know what it was all about and were scared to death of it.

We used to sit and just look at each other, hardly breathing, not really knowing each other at all. He called me "Clarita" — he still spoke with a good deal of Spanish accent in those days, and I used to love to hear him say my name, it was so soft and sweet. Neither of us had much money, and we used to do all sorts of silly little things to have a good time, and we used to think it was wonderful when we could go out to dinner and to a theater.

I think we might have been happy together if outside things hadn't interfered so dreadfully. We were happy, for a year and a half, and used to talk about getting married, and the time when we'd both be stars.

Well, we're both stars now, but the rest of the dream has vanished, and like every girl, I look back on my first love with tender memories and maybe a tear, though I know it can never come again.

I don't know just what separated us, but Gilbert was working hard on one lot and I on another, and everyone came between us, and we were both very jealous. And at last we had a violent quarrel. I don't think either of us meant it, or dreamed it would be final. But it went on and on, and we were both too proud to make the first move, so the breach finally grew so wide and we were so far apart that we never made it up.

Mrs. Smith had been doing a lot of odd things about my business affairs. She kept trying to make me think that I wasn't making good and that they were going to send me back to New York very soon. I worried about that all the time, and gave her more and more authority and power, because I thought she might keep them from doing that.

Finally, my Dad came West. Mrs. Smith had done a lot of things to make me think that Dad wasn't what he should be and that he would handicap me in a business way. She said relatives always did and that it would make the bosses sore around the studios if my father came interfering. I believed her. I knew so little about things, and what with working the whole time and trying to enjoy myself in spare moments I was — just dumb, I guess.

When Daddy arrived I had quite made up my mind to leave him out of things and to show him at once that he must not interfere with this great "career" that seemed opening up before me. I felt that perhaps he actually would be out of the picture and — oh, I am ashamed to tell this, but it came out all right and perhaps will make you understand a little of what I went through — when he arrived I was going to be very cool and aloof with him. I was now a successful motion picture actress and I intended to keep my new position and put him in his place.

When we met I just said, "Hello, Dad," and looked at him. I had on a new frock and, maybe, a new personality. I had learned so much about personality in the months I had been in Hollywood. I had been seeing the world and getting my first taste of success and admiration and money. I had begun to stand out a little, to hear people say, "That's Clara Bow. They say she's very clever."

Dad just stood and looked at me. He looked a little tired and worn, as though he had been working very hard. But as he looked the light went out of his face, the light and joy and welcome that had been his at seeing his little daughter again.

And suddenly I couldn't do it. I didn't care a — a rap, for Mrs. Smith, nor B.P. Shulberg, nor my motion picture career, nor Clara Bow. I just threw myself into his arms and kissed and kissed him, and we both cried like a couple of fool kids. Oh, it was wonderful. I knew then how lonely I had been for someone of my own, someone who belonged to me and really loved me.

We sat down and had a long talk, and right away Dad started looking into all these things. And soon I knew that Mrs. Smith hadn't told me the truth at all. She knew that the work I had done was very successful and that they liked me very much. But she wanted to keep a hold on me so she made me think I wasn't getting over and that nothing but her clever management kept me going.

***

About this time Frank Lloyd, the great director, was looking for a girl to play the flapper in *Black Oxen*. He had looked at everybody almost on the screen and tested them, but he had not found exactly what he wanted and finally somebody suggested me to him. I shall never forget the kind way he received me. He didn't do as most people had done in Hollywood, try to make me think I didn't have a chance and that they were doing me a favor when they let me work in their pictures. When I came into his office a big smile came over his face and he looked just tickled to death. And he told me instantly that I was just what he wanted.

Of all the people in motion pictures, I owe the most to Frank Lloyd, for the chance he gave me to establish myself as the screen flapper in *Black Oxen*, for the direction he gave me which showed me entirely new vistas in screen acting — and to Elinor Glyn, for the way she taught me to bring out my personality, and the way she concentrated her great word "It" upon me.

All this time I was "running wild," I guess, in the sense of trying to have a good time. I'd never had any fun in my life, as you know. And I was just a kid, under twenty, with a background of grief and poverty that I've tried to make you understand, even though I've had to bare my whole soul to do it. Why, I'd never been to a real party, a real dance. I'd never had a beautiful dress to wear, never had anyone send me flowers. It was like a new world to me, and I just drank it all in with that immense capacity of youth for understanding and loving excitement, I tried to make up for all my barren, hungry, starved-for-beauty years in no time at all.

Maybe this was a good thing, because I suppose a lot of that excitement, that joy of life, got onto the screen, and was the sort of flame of youth that made people enjoy seeing me. A philosopher might call it the swing of the pendulum, from my early years of terror and lack, to this time when all the pleasures of the world opened before me.

Just about this time, I met Victor Fleming, who directed me in several pictures.

Victor Fleming is a wonderful man. You have no idea how wonderful he is because the public scarcely knows about directors at all. But he is a man, older a great deal than I am, and very strong. He knows the world, he has cultivated a great sense of values through living, and he is deeply cultured. I liked him at once, though I didn't feel in the least romantic about him.

But soon we became great friends and he had a tremendous and very fine influence on my life. He grew fond of me at once. And he began, with his strong intellect and understanding of life, to guide me in little ways. He showed me that life must be lived, not just for the moment, but for the years. He showed me what a future I might have as an actress, because I had made a place for myself that people seemed to want. He was very patient, and he taught me a great deal. He formed a lot of ideas that were running around in my mind.

Mr. Schulberg had gone into Paramount and taken my contract, which he had signed a while before, with him. So I was working for Paramount, and they were beginning to do things for me and I could see that I was important to them. It looked as though if I made good in the chances they gave me I would be a big star. So I began at that time to be subject to flattery, to people who had never paid any attention to me coming around to tell me how wonderful I was, to getting a salary that I didn't in the least know how to spend or invest.

Under all this, I used to feel a little lost. I'd wake up in the morning and, like the old woman in the nursery rhyme, I'd wonder if this "could be really I." I think that sense of things kept me from ever getting fatheaded, as the youngsters I know say. But it all had to be coped with.

And in this crisis I learned to find the advice and companionship of a man like Victor Fleming invaluable. You couldn't deceive him with any false glitter. He steered me straight a lot of times when I was going "haywire."

And gradually our friendship seemed to deepen until it became the great thing in both our lives. I think he cared for me because he knew how much I wanted to get happiness out of life, and yet how frightened, in a way, I was of it, — and still am for that matter. Life has been so good to me. And yet, even now, with all I see before me, I cannot quite trust life.

It did too may awful things to me in my youth. I still feel that I must beat it, grab everything quickly, enjoy the moment to the utmost, because to-morrow, life may bludgeon me down, as it did my mother, as it used to do to the people I lived with in Brooklyn when I was a kid.

I had had a pretty good education, in spite of lacks in other ways, and while Victor Fleming and I were engaged — we became engaged about that time — I began to read again, and to enjoy music, and to grow calmer about many things.

I was very happy. I was gradually growing more and more successful in my work. I loved it. There is one thing I must say about my work as a picture star. I have worked very hard. I've been at the studio terribly long hours. I've had very little time between pictures. It would probably amaze anyone to see how much of my life the last four years has been spent on a motion picture set. But I've loved it.

Perhaps the difference in age brought about the severing of the tie be-tween Victor Fleming and me, though we are still the best of friends. Per-haps the feeling I had grown so gradually and under such circumstances that there wasn't quite enough romance in it. I was young and I needed romance. Perhaps even he found that I didn't give him the sort of com-panionship he needed.

Anyway, our feeling for each other became more and more that of close friendship and less and less that of lovers. Until finally we agreed that it would be best that way, to be friends, nothing more.

***

Right after that, while I was making a picture once more with my dear Frank Lloyd, a picture called *Children of Divorce*, I met a young man named Gary Cooper. It was his first big part — he'd been a cowboy up in

Nevada or something and played a small part in some Western picture. He was to play the lead. Of course he was new to the screen and didn't know exactly how to do things, though he was wonderful and photographed marvelously. I always like to help anyone who is new, so I was willing to go over and over scenes with him, in rehearsal, to help him out.

While we were doing that, we fell in love. If I wanted to be the Clara Bow of the screen, I'd say — and how! It was very wonderful and beautiful while it lasted. But — I can't altogether explain. It's very difficult to be a motion picture star and be married. So many fail at it. I have made up my mind that I shan't fail when I do marry. I shall wait until I'm sure. Gary was — so jealous. I know he wouldn't mind my saying that. Anyway, we parted.

Is that so many romances for a girl of twenty-two? Haven't most girls been engaged two or three times, before they're twenty-two? Yet just because I am Clara Bow and it is always printed, it sounds as though I were a regular flapper vamp. And I'm not at all.

It seems to me I've said very little about my career, after I became successful. But the story of every success is much the same. You work and suffer and battle and starve, and then you get your nose in a little way and then — you get the break. And if you have it in you, you make good. And then you just go on working, getting more money and loving the fame and the admiration of the public.

Somehow, I had managed to make a niche for myself. I'd created a Clara Bow by being myself largely I guess, who fitted the public desire and the public imagination. I hope they'll go on loving me a long time. I don't know.

I live in my little bungalow in Beverly Hills with my father. I work very, very hard. I like young people and gaiety, and have a lot of both around me whenever I have time. I like to swim and ride and play tennis.

I have a few close friends, but not many acquaintances. I don't have time. I am happy — as happy as anyone can be who believes that life isn't quite to be trusted. I give everything I can to my pictures and the rest to being young and trying to make my father happy, and filling up the gaps in my education.

I don't think I'm very different from any other girl — except that I work harder and have suffered more. And I have red hair.

All in all, I guess I'm just Clara Bow. And Clara Bow is just what life made her. That's what I've tried to tell you in this story. I'm terribly grateful and still a little incredulous of my success. It seems like a dream. But — I'm willing to work just as hard as ever to go on having it. Beyond that, I haven't yet evolved any plans or desires.

After all, I'm still only twenty-two. That isn't so very old, is it?

Promotional photo for the 1930 film *True to the Navy*, starring actress Clara Bow.

618-B

CLARA BOW "HER WEDDING NIGHT"

A Paramount Picture

CLARA BOW in HOOPLA

Clara Bow
An ELINOR GLYN~CLARENCE BADGER
Production
"IT"
with
ANTONIO MORENO
A Paramount Picture

REFLECTIONS ON MOTHERHOOD

As told to Jewel Smith

I suppose every mother has spent months figuring on what she would tell her first child. I know I am no different from all others, but each one figures from her own experiences. And there, I believe I have a right to think I am different. Not many mothers have had exactly the same experiences. I'm pretty sure no other mother has had mine or anything like it. So what I tell my child will be based upon things that haven't happened to other people.

First, I take this very seriously. All my life I have wanted a baby and now that I'm going to have one I realize I have to be very careful what I do with it – especially what I say to it. Because I lost my own mother so young. I know that no one else can ever take her place. You can have a dozen husbands ; you can have more children if anything happens to one. But you can never have but one mother.

You've read how lonesome I've always been. I used to tell how I wanted to marry a man who would stroke my hair and talk softly and let me tell him things. I remember the first time I read an interview I'd given about that. I went to bed with the magazine under my pillow and cried myself to sleep.

I was too young and too emotional to understand just why I wanted that kind of a husband. I do know. I know I was hunting a man who would be a mother even more than a husband. I wanted someone to confide in ; to cry to – someone who would sympathize and understand me no matter what I did. I thought that was a husband I know, now, it was a mother.

Motherhood Serious to Clara

The first thing I am going to tell a child, whether it's a boy or a girl is that he has a mother. I'm going to make myself sort of a safety valve for that baby from the very beginning. Whenever it cries, from the very first, I'm going to be the one it sees standing over the cradle. A nurse may be there too. A nurse may give him his bottle or change the pins and do the practical things that must be done for a baby. But that baby is not going to look into nurse's eyes for sympathy and understanding. He's going to look into his mother's. That's the reason making another picture isn't as important as it used to be. I wouldn't make one if it interfered with my being with my baby. That baby is going to know, from the very first breath he draws, that he's more important to me than work or bridge or women's clubs or anything else that keeps mothers busy.

I know a lot of people think a woman like me won't make a good mother. They probably think, "God help that child." That's where people are wrong. Girls like me make the best mothers, if we have any common sense. We know about things and you can only help your children from what you know. I've been reading a lot of books on taking care of children. I've had a lot of laughs from them. What do professors and nurses, who haven't loved and laughed and cried and suffered and starved and spent thousands of dollars really know about living? You's think from what I've read that all babies have is bodies. Well, I know different. It's a child's souls, his thoughts, that are the most important.

Clara's Careful Plans

I've been reading recently a lot about too much love giving children mother complexes. And I think that's a lot of bunk. Of course, there is two kinds of mother love.

One is done because the mother is selfish. She says "I love you so much you have to do what I say." I can understand how that kind of love might ruin a kid. It isn't real love. It's love for the mother rather than the baby. Mine won't be that kind. It'll be the kind that just says, " I love you. You know that. No matter what you do, whether you cry, whether you fight, whether you get into mischief, whether you get married to the right girl or to the wrong, whether you become a big, honest man or whether you happen to get into prison accidently or on purpose, there's one person you can always trust to love you. And that's your mother. And if he understands that – I don't think he'll be as apt to have bad luck.

That goes for a boy or a girl, but from then on things are different.

An Honest Education

HE'S even going to understand there are good snakes that you mustn't kill, poisonous ones you step on the second you see 'em. And he's going to be told humans are about the same! "If you can learn to tell a kind snake from the poisonous one, you can learn to tell a kind human from a poisonous one in the same way. Be good to the good ones and step on the others. Step on them before they get a chance to step on you!"

There isn't going to be anything left for him to find out if I can help it when he's ready to step into the world and fight his own battle. If he wants to fight his own battle. If he wants to fight when he's going to school and he's got common sense enough to pick the mean ones to fight, he's going to be encouraged. I'll tell him "Okay, that was a bad snake. You did right to step on it." But he's got to pick his own snakes! I'm not going to take the initiative and wisdom out of him by trying to pick 'em for him.

And I hope he knows women well enough, by the time he's ready to marry, so he'll understand them the same way. To do that he's got to mix with snakes on the ranch to tell a rattler from a gopher. There'd be no sense in trying to keep him from it, anyway, because I know men. They are always men. Men are about the same now as they were when Cleopatra was playing with her generals. And for a mother to think she's going to create a new kind is foolish.

I'm glad I'm not a very wealthy woman. My boy will know there's enough to help him from having to make some of his own. If he knows that from the beginning he's going to start using part of the energy and brains God gave him to think about it. He'll make his own choice there. He'll know I'm standing behind him but he'll know, too, it's his life, and I can't live it for him.

Girls Must Have Romance

WHEN it comes to a girl – I'm not so sure. As I see it, the place of women hasn't been exactly decided. It's a tough time to raise a girl. I suppose that's one reason why I sort of hope it'll be a boy. I see Mussolini is putting the ladies back into the home to do the cooking, read families, and care for their men. And although, I've worked most of my life, I sort of think that Mussolini must have decided God knows more than he does about that matter. After all, it was God who decided about women in the first place, wasn't it?

You see, I'm a girl and I know that there's nothing as important to a girl as romance. And since romance is so important, you've got to be very careful not to take it away from your daughter.

I hope I can send my daughter to private schools and dress her in dainty dresses and have her learn how to play the piano and sew. I'm going to teach my daughter to be a dainty lady. I tell you a woman isn't created physically to stand strain of a career. In the business world you are apt to be brought into suits, for example. A woman's emotions rule her feelings. She carries her emotions into a court room instead of her common sense or brains. She can't help it. She shouldn't help it. Woman was made to feel and man to think. I want my daughter to have the chance to live as God intended. Woman cannot struggle and battle and compete – she shouldn't have to.

I have been called over-emotional. I suppose I am. That's a compliment to a woman. It should be. But it's not good in the business world. I'm called impulsive. I am. But that's a drawback, too, when you're working. Of course, if my daughter wanted to work, wanted a screen career for example, I wouldn't stop her. I wouldn't have the right. It's her life.

I guess I'm a little old-fashioned but I think most girls who have lived life, as I have, get old-fashioned when they are old enough to see happiness is all you want here. Glory and fame, even money, don't bring happiness. And, in the long run, I only want my child to be happy!

CLARA BOW FILMOGRAPHY

BEYOND THE RAINBOW (EXTANT)
(Robertson-Cole, 1922), 6,000'

Director: William Christy Cabanne
Based on the story "The Price of Feathers" by Solita Solano
Screenplay: William Christy Cabanne, Loila Brooks
Art director, Frank Campury
Camera: William Tirers, Philip Armand.

Cast: Harry Morey (Edward Mallory); Lillian "Billie" Dove (Marion Taylor); Virginia Lee (Henrietta Greeley); Diana Allen (Frances Gardener); James Harrison (Louis Wade); Macey Harlam (Count Julien de Brisac); Rose Coghlan (Mrs. Burns); William Tooker (Dr. Ramsey); Helen Ware (Mrs. Gardener); George Fawcett (Mr. Gardener); Marguerite Courtot (Esther); Edmund Breese (Inspector Richardson); Walter Miller (Robert Mason); Charles Craig (Col. Henry Gartwright); **Clara Bow (Virginia Gardener)**; Huntley Gordon (Bruce Forbes).

Synopsis: Clara Bow appears as Virginia Gardener, a bright presence amid a tangle of romantic misunderstandings and upper-class intrigue. Contemporary reviews suggest she injected youthful spontaneity into an otherwise conventional melodrama. Her role adds momentum to the plot's emotional conflicts, and even in this early appearance she reportedly displayed the expressive vivacity that would later define her screen persona. Surviving production notes highlight that Bow stood out despite limited screen time, marking the first signs of her magnetic appeal.

DOWN TO THE SEA IN SHIPS (EXTANT)
(Hodkinson, 1922) 12 reels

Presenter-director: Elmer Clifton
Story-screenplay: John L. E. Pell
Music score designed by Henry F. Gilbert
Camera: Alexander G. Penrod.

Cast: William Walcott (William W. Morgan); William Cavanaugh (Henry Morgan); Ada Laycock (Henny Clark); Leigh R. Smith ("Scuff" Smith); Marguerite Courtot (Patience Morgan);.Raymond McKee (Thomas Allen Dexter); Juliette Courtot (Judy Peggs); Clarice Vance (Nahoma); Curtis Pierce (Town Crier); **Clara Bow ("Dot" Morgan)**; Patrick Hartigan (Jake Finner); J. Thornton Baston (Samuel Siggs); James Turfler (Cabin Boy), Captain James A. Tilton (Captain of the "Morgan"); Elizabeth Fuley (Patience as a child); Thomas White (Tommy as a child).

Synopsis: Bow plays Dot Morgan, a lively young woman in a whaling community, providing warmth and humor in a story dominated by rugged maritime tradition. Her natural, unforced acting drew critical attention and distinguished her from the more theatrical performers around her. The character's spirited presence offsets the film's grittier sequences and helps humanize its portrayal of New England life. This was a landmark early role: audiences and critics alike singled Bow out as a refreshing new screen talent.

THE PILL POUNDER (EXTANT)
(W.W. Hodkinson Corporation, 1923), 2 reels

Producer: C.C. Burr
Director: Gregory La Cava
Cinematography: Charles E. Gilson
Production Company: All Star Comedies

Cast: Charles Murray, Clara Bow, James Turfler.

Synopsis: In this recently rediscovered two-reel comedy, Bow appears as a playful young woman whose presence causes chaos for a mild-mannered drugstore clerk. The film relies on fast-paced physical humor, and Bow's performance supplies the spark that drives many of its gags. Even at this early stage of her career, she demonstrates the confident timing and expressive face that would soon become her trademarks. Thanks to the recent rediscovery of a surviving print, this short now provides a rare glimpse of Bow's comedic instincts during her earliest screen years.

THE DARING YEARS (LOST FILM)
(Equity, 1923) 6,702'

Producer: Daniel Carson Goodman
Director: Kenneth Webb
Story-screenplay: Daniel Carson Goodman

Cast: Mildred Harris (Susie La Motte); Charles Emmett Mack (John Browning); **Clara Bow (John's Sweetheart, Mary)**; Mary Carr (Mrs. Browning); Joe King (Jim Moran, a Pugilist); Tyrone Power (James La Motte); Skeets Gallagher (The College Boy); Jack Richardson (Flaglier, Cabaret Owner); Sherman Sisters (Moran Girls); Joseph Depew, Helen Rowland (La Motte's Kids); Sam Sidman (Curly, Moran's Manager).

Synopsis: Bow plays Mary, the devoted sweetheart of a college athlete falsely accused of murder. Her character brings emotional clarity to the film's drama, serving as the unwavering moral anchor in a plot full of betrayal, violence, and courtroom suspense. Contemporary reviews noted her sincerity and brightness, which softened the film's darker elements. Though the feature does not survive, Bow's performance was frequently cited as a highlight in an otherwise somber melodrama.

ENEMIES OF WOMEN (EXTANT IN FRAGMENTARY FORM)
(Cosmopolitan, 1923) 10,501'

Director: Alan Crosland
Based on the novel by Vicente Blasco Ibanez
Screenplay: John Lynch
Camera: Ira Morgan.

Cast: Lionel Barrymore (Prince Lubimoff); Alma Rubens (Alicia); Pedro De Cordoba (Atilio Castro); Gareth Hughes (Spadoni); Gladys Hulette (Vittoria); William H. Thompson (Colonel Marcos); William Collier, Jr. (Gaston); Mario Majeroni (Duke De Delille); **Clara Bow (Girl Dancing on Table)**; Betty Bouton (Alicia's Maid); Madame Jean (Madame Spadoni); Ivan Linow (Terrorist); Paul Panzer (Cossack).

Synopsis: Bow appears in a small but memorable cameo as a dancer, injecting a burst of modern energy into a story centered on disillusioned aristocrats and their romances. Her brief appearance contrasts with the film's more formal tone, embodying the liberated 1920s spirit that she would later personify. Though on screen only moments, she made a vivid impression, and archival prints preserve her earliest surviving glimpse as a rising star.

MAYTIME (EXTANT IN FRAGMENTARY FORM)
(Preferred, 1923) 7,500'

Producer: B.P. Schulberg
Director: Louis A. Gasnier
Based on the operetta by Rida Johnson Young, Cyrus Wood, Sigmund Romberg
Adaptation, Olga Printzlau
Camera, Karl Struss.

Cast: Ethel Shannon (Ottilie Van Zandt); Harrison Ford (Richard Wayne); William Norris (Matthew); **Clara Bow (Alice Tremaine)**; Wallace MacDonald (Claude Van Zandt); Josef Swickard (Col. Van Zandt); Martha Mattox (Mathilda); Betty Francisco (Ermintrude); Robert McKim (Monte Mitchell).

Synopsis: As Alice Tremaine, Bow contributes youthful vitality to this adaptation of the beloved operetta. The film weaves together themes of long-delayed love and generational conflict, with Bow's character serving as a lively counterbalance to the more solemn main storyline. Her expressive reactions and spirited presence give the narrative a modern edge despite its old-world sentimental roots. Surviving prints confirm she brought significant screen life to her supporting role.

BLACK OXEN (EXTANT)
(Frank Lloyd Productions, 1924) 7,937'

Director: Frank Lloyd
Based on the novel by Gertrude Atherton
Camera: Norbert Brodine.

Cast: Corinne Griffith (Madame Zatianny/Mary Ogden); Conway Tearle (Lee Clavering); Thomas Ricketts (Charles Dinwiddie); Thomas S. Guise (Judge Trent); **Clara Bow (Janet Oglethorpe)**; Kate Lester (Jane Oglethorpe); Harry Mestayer (James Oglethorpe); Claire MacDowell (Agnes Trevor); Alan Hale (Prince Rohenhauer); Clarissa Selwynne (Gora Dwight), Fred Gambold (Oglethorpe's Butler); Percy Williams (Ogden's Butler); Otto Nelson (Dr. Steinach); Eric Mayne (Chancellor); Otto Lederer (Austrian Advisor); Carmelita Geraghty (Anna Goodrich); Ione Atkinson, Mila Constantin, Hortense O'Brien (Flappers).

Synopsis: Bow plays Janet Oglethorpe, a quintessential flapper whose energy symbolizes the modern world encroaching on an older generation's anxieties. In a plot centered on rejuvenation and identity, Bow's character represents youth in full stride — impulsive, stylish, and confident. Her scenes crackle with contemporary rhythm and sharply delineate the cultural divide driving the film's drama. The film survives in excellent condition, making this one of the earliest accessible examples of her flapper persona.

THIS WOMAN (EXTANT)
(Warner Brothers, 1924) 6,842'

Director: Phil Rosen
Based on the novel by Howard Rockey
Adaptation, Hope Loring, Louis Leighton
Camera, Lyman Broening

Cast: Irene Rich (Carol Drayton); Ricardo Cortez (Whitney Duane); Louise Fazenda (Rose); Frank Elliott (Gordon Duane); Creighton Hale (Bobby Bleedon); Marc McDermott (Stratini); Helen Dunbar (Mrs. Sturdevant); **Clara Bow (Aline Sturdevant)**; Otto Hoffman (Judson).

Synopsis: Bow appears as Aline Sturdevant, whose youthful warmth offsets the story of a woman wrongly accused of theft and scandal. Contemporary summaries describe Bow's performance as spirited and engaging, providing emotional texture within the household where much of the tension unfolds. Though her role was secondary, she was frequently mentioned in reviews for her bright screen presence.

GRIT (LOST FILM)
(Hodkinson, 1924) 5,800'

Director: Frank Tuttle
Story: F. Scott Fitzgerald.

Screenplay: Ashmore Creelman
Camera: Fred Waller, Jr.

Cast: Glenn Hunter ("Kid" Hart); Helenka Adamowska (Annie Hart); Roland Young (Houdini Hart); Osgood Perkins (Boris Giovanni Smith); Townsend Martin (Flashy Joe); **Clara Bow (Orchid McGonigle)**; Dore Davidson (Pop Finkel); Martin Borden (Bennie Finkel); Joseph Depew (Tony O'Cohen).

Synopsis: As Orchid McGonigle, Bow gives life to the street-smart girl who becomes part of a young man's struggle to escape criminal surroundings. Based loosely on a story by F. Scott Fitzgerald, the film blends underworld grit with romance, and Bow's performance embodies the carefree modernity that separates her from the film's darker characters. Although the film is lost, contemporary reviews praise her scenes for injecting warmth and immediacy into the narrative, helping elevate a modest production into a showcase for her rising talent.

POISONED PARADISE (EXTANT)
(Preferred, 1924) 6,800'

Producer: B.P. Schulberg.
Director: Louis Gasnier.
Based on the novel Poisoned Paradise: A Romance of Monte Carlo *by Robert W. Service*
Screenplay: Waldemar Young
Camera: Karl Struss

Cast: Kenneth Harlan (Hugh Kildair); **Clara Bow (Margot Le Blanc)**; Barbara Tennant (Mrs. Kildair); Andre de Beranger (Krantz); Carmel Myers (Mrs. Belmire); Raymond Griffith (Martel); Josef Swickard (Professor Durand); Evelyn Selbie (Mde. Tranquille).

Synopsis: Bow stars as Margot Le Blanc, a young woman caught in the seductive world of Monte Carlo. Her performance mixes innocence with determination, creating a character who navigates temptation without losing her emotional grounding. Opposite Kenneth Harlan, she brings vibrancy and sincerity to the romantic storyline, and her luminous screen presence was widely praised. Surviving materials confirm this as one of her first fully realized leading roles.

DAUGHTERS OF PLEASURE (EXTANT IN FRAGMENTARY FORM)
(Principal, 1924) 6 reels

Director: William Beaudine
Based on the story by Caleb Proctor
Screenplay, Eve Unsell
Titles: Harvey Thew
Art director, Joseph Wright
Camera: Charles van Enger
Editor: Edward McDermott.

Cast: Marie Prevost (Marjory Hadley); Monte Blue (Kent Merrill); **Clara Bow (Lila Millas)**; Edythe Chapman (Mrs. Hadley); Wilfred Lucas (Mark Hadley).

Synopsis: In this society melodrama, Clara Bow plays Lila Millas, a spirited young woman navigating the ambitions and emotional entanglements of a wealthy family caught between old-fashioned respectability and the temptations of modern life. As tensions rise around a romantic scandal that threatens the Hadley household, Lila serves as both confidante and instigator, her energy pushing the story toward its revelations. Although the film survives only in fragmentary form, contemporary reviews describe

Bow as a standout presence who injected vitality and lightness into a largely conventional morality tale.

WINE (LOST FILM)
(Universal Pictures, 1924) 6,220'

Director, Louis Gasnier
Based on the story by William MacHarg
Adaptation: Raymond L. Schrock
Screenplay, Philip Lonergan, Eve Unsell.

Cast: Clara Bow (Angela Warriner); Forrest Stanley (Carl Graham); Huntley Gordon (John Warriner); Myrtle Steadman (Mrs. Warriner); Robert Agnew (Harry Van Alstyne); Walter Long (Benedict, Count Montebello); Grace Carlyle (Mrs. Bruce Corwin); Leo White (The Duke); Walter Shumway (Revenue Officer); Arthur Thalasso (Amati).

Synopsis: Clara Bow stars as Angela Warriner, the rebellious daughter of a socially prominent family whose flirtation with bootlegging culture draws her into danger during the Prohibition era. The story follows Angela's bold attempts to assert her independence, only to find herself out of her depth when her involvement with alcohol smugglers forces a reckoning at home. Bow's performance reportedly emphasized Angela's mix of charm and impulsive bravado, and the film's publicity leaned heavily on her rising reputation as a modern, unconventional heroine. No known copies survive.

EMPTY HEARTS (LOST FILM)
(Banner, 1924) 6 reels

Producer: Ben Verschleiser
Director: Al Santell
Story: Evelyn Campbell

Screenplay: Adele Buffinton
Camera, Ernest Hallen.

Cast: John Bowers (Milt Kimberlin); Charles Murrey (Joe Delane); John Miljan (Frank Gorman); **Clara Bow (Rosalie)**; Lilian Rich (Madeline); Joan Standing (Hilda, The Maid); Buck Black (Val Kimberlin).

Synopsis: Bow appears as Rosalie, a young woman entangled in a story of jealousy and deception surrounding a strained marriage. When suspicion and misunderstanding pull the characters toward tragedy, Rosalie becomes a pivotal figure whose choices expose the fragility of the relationships around her. Though the film itself has been lost, accounts from its release suggest Bow brought emotional immediacy to a role that might otherwise have been overshadowed by the film's darker themes.

HELEN'S BABIES (EXTANT)
(Principal, 1925) 5,620'

Director: William A. Seiter
Based on the story by John Habberton
Adaptation: Hope Loring, Louis Leighton
Camera: William Daniels
Editor: Owen Marks.

Cast: Baby Peggy (Toddie); Jean Carpenter (Budge); **Clara Bow (Alice Mayton)**; Edward Everett Horton (Uncle Harry); Claire Adams (Helen Lawrence); Richard Tucker (Tom Lawrence); George Reed (Rastus, The Coachman); Mattie Peters (Mandy, The Housekeeper).

Synopsis: In this lighthearted comedy, Clara Bow plays Alice Mayton, a charming neighbor whose presence complicates the life of an inexperienced bachelor tasked with caring for two mischievous little girls. As the children create chaos and the bachelor struggles to maintain control, Alice becomes both a romantic foil and a stabilizing influence. Bow's warm, lively performance provides much of the film's appeal, and the picture survives in accessible form.

BLACK LIGHTNING (EXTANT)
(Gotham, 1924) 5,500'

Presenter: Samuel Sax
Director: James P. Hogan
Story: Harry Davis
Screenplay: Dorothy Howell
Camera, James P. Hogan

Cast: Clara Bow (Martha Larned); Harold Austin (Roy Chambers); Eddie Phillips (Ez Howard); James Mason (Jim Howard); Joe Butterworth (Larned); Mark Fenton (Doctor); John Prince (City Doctor); J. P. Hogan (Frank Larned); Thunder The Dog (Himself); Joe Butterworth (Dick).

Synopsis: Clara Bow portrays Martha Larned, the loyal daughter in a family caught up in a crime drama centered on a heroic police dog named Thunder. When tensions escalate between local criminals and the Larned household, Martha's courage and devotion play a key role in the unfolding conflict. Period write-ups singled out Bow's sincerity in a supporting role that gave her moments of emotional weight.

CAPITAL PUNISHMENT (EXTANT)
(Preferred, 1925) 5,950'

Producer: B. P. Schulberg
Art director: James P. Hogan
Story: B.P. Schulberg
Adaptation: John Goodrich
Titles: Florence L. Gilbert

Technical director: Frank Ormston;
Camera: John Goodrich.

Cast: Clara Bow (Delia Tate); George Hackathorne (Dan O'Connor); Elliott Dexter (Gordon Harrington); Margaret Livingston (Mona Caldwell); Alec B. Francis (Chaplain); Mary Carr (Mrs. O'Connor); Robert Ellis (Harry Phillip); Joseph Kilgour (Governor); George Nichols (Warden); Eddie Phillips (Condemned Boy); Edith Yorke (Boy's Mother); John Prince (Doctor); Wade Boteler (Officer Dugan); Fred Warren (Pawnbroker); Sailor Sharkey (Convict); Harry Tenbrook (Executioner).

Synopsis: As Delia Tate, Clara Bow appears in a somber drama about a young man wrongfully condemned to death and the desperate struggle to save him. Delia's personal connection to the case drives much of the emotional urgency, with Bow contributing a sympathetic portrayal that reinforced her growing reputation for expressive, camera-conscious acting. Audiences at the time praised the film's intensity.

THE ADVENTUROUS SEX (LOST FILM)
(Associated Exhibitors, 1925) 5,039'

Director: Charles Giblyn
Story: Hamilton Mannen
Screenplay: Carl Stearns Clancy
Camera: George Peters.

Cast: Clara Bow (The Girl); Herbert Rawlinson (Her Sweetheart); Earle Williams (The Adventurer); Harry T. Morey (Her Father); Mabel Beck (Her Mother); Flora Finch (The Grandmother); and: Joseph Burke.

Synopsis: This romantic drama casts Bow as an unnamed young woman whose romantic entanglements become complicated by an adventurous stranger. Her character serves as the emotional center of the story, torn between loyalty and the thrill of the unknown. While little documentation remains, trade summaries praised Bow for infusing the part with her characteristic vibrancy. The film is believed lost.

EVE'S LOVER (LOST FILM)
(WB, 1925) 7,237'

Director: Roy Del Ruth
Story: Mrs. W. K. Clifford
Adaptation: Darryl F. Zanuck
Camera, George Winkler.

Cast: Irene Rich (Eva Burnside); Bert Lytell (Baron Geraldo Maddox); **Clara Bow (Rena D'Arcy)**; Willard Louis (Austin Starfield); John Steppling (Burton Gregg); Arthur Hoyt (Amos Potts); Lew Harvey (The Agitator).

Synopsis: Clara Bow plays Rena D'Arcy, a spirited supporting character who adds liveliness to a drama involving marital discord, social intrigue, and romantic temptation. Rena's mischievous energy provides contrast to the more serious dramatic plot surrounding a woman caught between two men. Reviews from the period noted Bow's ability to steal scenes despite limited screen time. The film does not survive.

THE LAWFUL CHEATER (LOST FILM)
(Preferred Pictures, 1925) 4,898'

Producer: B.P. Schulberg
Director: Frank O'Connor
Adaptation: Adele Buffington
Screenplay: O'Connor.

Cast: Clara Bow (Molly Burns); David Kirby (Rooney) Raymond McKee (Richard Steele); Edward Hearn (Roy Burns); George Cooper (Johnny Burns); Fred Kelsey (Tom Horan); Gertrude Pedlar (Mrs. Perry Steele); Jack Wise (Graveyard Lazardi); John T. Prince (Silent Sam Riley).

Synopsis: As Molly Burns, Bow takes on the role of a streetwise young woman drawn into a web of family loyalty, petty crime, and hard choices. The story follows Molly as she attempts to help her brothers navigate the consequences of their actions while asserting her own sense of right and wrong. Contemporary reports emphasized Bow's naturalism in portraying a character shaped by tough circumstances. The film is lost.

THE SCARLET WEST (LOST FILM)
(FN, 1925) 8,390'

Producer: Frank J. Carroll
Director: John G. Adolfi
Based on the story by A. B. Heath
Screenplay: Anthony Paul Kelly
Camera: George Benoit, Benjamin Kline, Victor Shuler; F.L. Hoefler.

Cast: Robert Edeson (General Kinnard); Martha Francis (Harriet Kinnard); **Clara Bow (Miriam)**; Johnnie Walker (Lt. Parkman); Walter McGrail (Lt. Harper); Florence Crawford (Mrs. Harper); Robert Frazer (Cardelanche); Helen Ferguson (Nestina); Ruth Stonehouse (Mrs. Custer); Gaston Glass (Captain Howard).

Synopsis: Clara Bow appears as Miriam, a frontier woman caught amid personal rivalries and military conflict in a dramatic retelling of events surrounding General Custer. Miriam's interactions with soldiers and settlers place her at the emotional core of several key narrative threads. Bow's performance was often cited for its freshness amid an otherwise traditional historical drama. The film is considered lost.

MY LADY'S LIPS (EXTANT)
(Preferred, 1925) 6,609'

Producer: B.P. Schulberg
Director: James P. Hogan
Story-continuity: John Goodrich
Camera: Allen Siegler.

Cast: Clara Bow (Lola Lombard); Frank Keenan (Forbes Lombard); Alyce Mills (Dora Blake); William Powell (Scott Seddon): Ford Sterling (Smike); Gertrude Short (Crook Girl); John Sainpolis (Inspector); Matthew Betz (Eddie Gault); and Sojin.

Synopsis: Clara Bow stars as Lola Lombard, a captivating young woman tangled in a world of crime, undercover work, and divided loyalties. When an earnest reporter infiltrates her father's criminal gang, Lola is drawn between family obligation and her growing connection with him. Bow's performance brings a blend of toughness and vulnerability to the role, grounding the film's fast-paced action with genuine emotional stakes. A surviving print allows modern audiences to appreciate her early screen magnetism.

PARISIAN LOVE (EXTANT)
(Preferred, 1925) 6,324'

Producer: B.P. Schulberg
Director: Louis Gasnier
Story: F. Oakley Crawford
Adaptation: Lois Hutchinson
Camera: Allen Siegler.

Cast: Clara Bow (Marie); Donald Keith (Armand); Lillian Leighton (Frouchard); James Russell (D'Avril); Hazel Keener (Margot); Lou Tellegen (Pierre Marcel); Jean de Briac (Knifer); Otto Matieson (Apache Leader).

Synopsis: In one of her defining early roles, Bow plays Marie, a streetwise Parisian Apache girl whose loyalty and passion drive a tale of deception and class conflict. When she falls for a young man from a higher social world, Marie's plan to test his devotion spirals into danger and misunderstanding. Bow's portrayal combines fiery intensity with moments of raw tenderness, and the film survives intact, offering a vivid case study of her emerging star persona.

KISS ME AGAIN (EXTANT)
(Warner Brothers, 1925) 6,722'

Director: Ernst Lubitsch
Based on the play "Nous Divorcons"
Screenplay: Hans Kraly
Camera: Charles Van Enger

Cast: Marie Prevost (Loulou Fleury); Monte Blue (Gaston Fleury); John Roche (Maurice); **Clara Bow (Grisette)**; Willard Louis (Dr. Dubois).

Synopsis: Clara Bow appears as a mischievous grisette in this Lubitsch-directed operetta comedy about marital mix-ups, romantic flirtation, and the intricacies of Parisian domestic life. Though not the central figure, Bow enlivens the film with her light comic timing and sly expressiveness, adding sparkle to the ensemble. The film survives and showcases her ability to stand out even in smaller roles.

THE KEEPER OF THE BEES (EXTANT)
(FBO, 1925) 6,712'

Director: J. Leo Meeham
Based on the novel by Gene Stratton Porter
Continuity: Meehan
Assistant director: William Fisher
Camera: John Boyle.

Cast: Robert Frazer (James McFarlane); Josef Swickard (The Bee Master); Martha Maddox (Mrs. Cameron); **Clara Bow (Lolly Cameron)**; Alyce Mills (Molly Cameron); Gene Stratton (Little Scout);Joe Coppa ("Angel Face"); Billy Osborn ("Nice Child"); Ainse Charland ("Fat Ole Bill").

Synopsis: Bow portrays Lolly Cameron, a lively young woman whose warmth and curiosity influence the life of a returning war veteran seeking peace and renewal on a bee farm. While the story centers on themes of healing and nature, Lolly's vibrant presence injects humor and emotional color into the film. This title survives and offers an example of Bow's early ability to shift seamlessly between drama and lighthearted charm.

THE PRIMROSE PATH (LOST FILM)
(Arrow, 1925) 6,800'

Producer: Hunt Stromberg
Director: Harry O. Hoyt
Based on the novel by E. Lanning Masters
Screenplay: Leah Baird, Andre Barlatier

Cast: Clara Bow (Marilyn Merrill); Wallace MacDonald (Bruce Armstrong); Stuart Holmes (Tom Canfield); Templar Saxe (Dude Talbot); Lydia Knott (Mrs. Armstrong); Pat Moore (Jimmie Armstrong); Tom Santschi (Big Joe Snead); Arline Pretty (Helen); Mike Donlin (Parker,

Federal Officer); George Irving (John Morton, Prosecutor); Henry Hall (Court Officer).

Synopsis: As Marilyn Merrill, Clara Bow anchors this romantic drama about a young woman whose past mistakes threaten her chance at a new life. When Marilyn becomes entangled with conflicting suitors and criminal intrigue, Bow's performance reportedly emphasized the character's resolve and emotional complexity. Reviews from the period credit her with giving depth to a story shaped by moral tension. The film is lost.

FREE TO LOVE (LOST FILM)
(Preferred, 1925), 4,825'

Producer: B.P. Schulberg
Director: Frank O'Connor

Cast: Clara Bow (Marie Anthony); Donald Keith (Reverend James Crawford); Raymond McKee (Tony); Hallam Cooley (Jack Garner); Charles Mailes (Kenton Crawford); Winter Hall (Judge Orr).

Synopsis: Bow plays Marie Anthony, a young woman released from a reformatory who attempts to rebuild her life in the face of corruption and social prejudice. When a reform-minded minister believes in her potential and local criminals attempt to draw her back into danger, Marie's struggle becomes the heart of the story. Contemporary accounts noted Bow's sympathetic and sincere performance. No known prints survive.

THE BEST BAD MAN (EXTANT)
(FOX, 1925) 4,893'

Presenter: William Fox
Director: J.G. Blystone
Based on the story "Senor Jingle Bells" by Max Brand

Screenplay: Lillie Hayward
Assistant director: Jasper Blystone
Camera: Dan Clark

Cast: Tom Mix (Hugh Nichols); Buster Gardener (Hank Smith); Cyril Chadwick (Frank Dunlap); **Clara Bow (Peggy Swain)**; Tom Kennedy (Dan Ellis); Frank Beal (Mr. Swain); Judy King (Molly Jones); Tom Wilson (Sam); Tony The Wonder Horse (Himself); Paul Panzer (Sheriff); Tom Wilson (Sam The Butler).

Synopsis: In this western-tinged comedy-drama, Clara Bow plays Peggy Swain, the spirited daughter of a rancher caught in a feud between a benevolent outlaw and local villains. Peggy's impulsiveness and energy drive much of the conflict and charm, with Bow bringing youthful verve to the role. The film's mixture of action and light romance was praised on its release.

THE ANCIENT MARINER (LOST FILM)
(FOX, 1925) 5,548'

Director: Henry Bennett
Based on the poem "The Rime of the Ancient Mariner" by Samuel Taylor Coleridge
Story: Chester Barnett
Adaptation: Eve Unsell
Assistant director: James Tinling
Titles: Tom Miranda
Camera: Joseph August

Cast: Clara Bow (Doris); Matthews Earle Williams (Victor Brandt); Leslie Fenton (Joe Barlowe); Nigel de Brulier (Skipper); Paul Panzer (Mariner); Gladys Brockwell (Life In Death); Robert Klein (Death).

Synopsis: Clara Bow appears as Doris in this imaginative dramatization inspired by Coleridge's famous poem. Though the story departs significantly from the original text, Doris becomes a figure linked to the film's moral and supernatural themes, caught between sailors, superstition, and the mariner's curse. Bow's supporting role added brightness to an otherwise somber production. The film does not survive.

MY LADY OF WHIMS (EXTANT)
(Arrow, 1925) 6,089'

Director: Dallas M. Fitzgerald
Based on the story "Protecting Prue" by Edgar Franklin
Screenplay: Doris Schroeder
Camera, Jack Young

Cast: Clara Bow (Prudence Severn); Donald Keith (Bartley Greer); Carmelita Geraghty (Wayne Leigh); Lee Moran (Dick Flynn); Francis McDonald (Rolf); John Cossar (Severn); Robert Rose (Sneath); Lux MacBride (Yacht Captain); Betty Baker (Mary Severn).

Synopsis: Bow stars as Prudence Severn, a free-spirited young woman whose bohemian lifestyle in Greenwich Village alarms her conservative family. When they hire a man to watch over her, Prudence turns the situation into a battle of wills fueled by independence, flirtation, and comedic rebellion. Surviving prints allow viewers to see one of Bow's most charismatic early starring performances, full of wit and emotional clarity.

THE PLASTIC AGE (EXTANT)
(Preferred, 1925), 6,488'

Producer: B.P. Schulberg
Director: Wesley Ruggles
Based on the novel by Percy Marks

Adaptation: Eve Unsell, Frederica Sagor
Camera: Gilbert Warrenton, Allen Siegler

Cast: Clara Bow (Cynthia Day); Donald Keith (Hugh Carver); Mary Alden (Mrs. Carver); Henry B. Walthall (Henry Carver); Gilbert Roland (Carl Peters); J. Gordon Edwards, Jr. (Norrie Parks); David Butler (Coach Henley); Felix Valle (Merton Billings); Clark Gable (Athlete); Gordon "William" Elliott (Dancer); Churchill Ross (Boy with Glasses); Gwen Lee (Carl's Girl).

Synopsis: In this influential college drama, Clara Bow plays Cynthia Day, the vivacious campus "IT girl" whose charm, spontaneity, and emotional openness challenge a shy student striving to define himself. Cynthia functions as both temptation and catalyst, embodying the modern, youthful spirit of the 1920s. The film survives and remains one of Bow's most important early roles, cementing her as a rising star.

THE SHADOW OF THE LAW (LOST FILM)
(Associated Exhibitors, 1926) 4,526'

Producers: Arthur Beck, Leah Baird
Director: Wallace Worsley
Based on the novel "Two Gates" by Henry Chapman Ford
Screenplay: Leah Baird, Grover Jones
Camera: Ray June

Cast: Clara Bow (Mary Brophy); Forrest Stanley (James Reynolds); Stuart Holmes (Linyard); Ralph Lewis (Brophy); William V. Mong (Egan); J. Emmett Beck (Martin); Adele Farrington (Aunt); Eddie Lyons (Crook); George Cooper (Chauffeur).

Synopsis: Bow appears as Mary Brophy, a young woman whose loyalty to her father entangles her in a crime story marked by wrongful accusations and hidden motives. Mary's determination and quiet resilience serve as emotional anchors in a narrative shaped by corruption and injustice. Critics at the time singled out Bow's expressive presence in a role more restrained than many she would soon play. The film is lost.

TWO CAN PLAY (LOST FILM)
(Associated Exhibitors, 1926) 5,465'

Director: Nat Ross
Story: Gerald Mygatt
Screenplay: Reginald G. Fogwell
Camera: Andre Barlatier
Editor: Gene Milford

Cast: George Fawcett (John Hammis); Allan Forrest (James Radley); **Clara Bow (Dorothy Hammis)**; Wallace McDonald (Robert MacForth); Vola Vale (Mimi).

Synopsis: Clara Bow plays Dorothy Hammis, the spirited daughter of a wealthy man, whose romantic entanglements collide with a scheme involving deception and mistaken intentions. Dorothy's quick wit and emotional candor give the drama its liveliest moments, with Bow reportedly infusing the role with charm and energy. The film is now considered lost.

DANCING MOTHERS (EXTANT)
(Paramount, 1926) 7,169'

Producer: Herbert Brenon
Associate producer: William LeBaron
Director: Herbert Brenon
Based on the play by Edgar Selwyn, Edmund Goulding
Screenplay: Forrest Halsey

Art director: Julian Boone Fleming
Camera: J. Roy Hunt

Cast: Alice Joyce (Ethel "Buddy" Westcourt); Conway Tearle (Jerry Naughton); **Clara Bow (Catherine "Kittens" Westcourt)**; Donald Keith (Kenneth Cobb); Dorothy Cumming (Mrs. Mazzarene); Elsie Lawson (Irma Raymond); Norman Trevon (Hugh Westcourt); Leila Hyams (Birdie Courtney); Spencer Charters (Butter And Egg Man).

Synopsis: In one of her most acclaimed early performances, Bow plays Kittens Westcourt, a pleasure-seeking flapper whose impulsive lifestyle strains her family's stability. As her behavior pushes her mother toward a dramatic personal awakening, Kittens becomes the embodiment of youthful rebellion and the social tensions of the era. The film survives and is widely regarded as a key turning point in Bow's ascent to major stardom.

FASCINATING YOUTH (EXTANT)
(Paramount, 1926), [c. 6 reels]

Producers: Adolph Zukor, Jesse L. Lasky
Director: Sam Wood
Screenplay: Paul Schofield
Story: Byron Morgan
Cinematography: Leo Tover

Cast: Charles "Buddy" Rogers (Teddy Ward); Ivy Harris (Jeanne King); Jack Luden (Ross Page); Walter Goss (Randy Furness) Claude Buchanan (Bobby Stearns); Mona Palma (Dotty Sinclair); Thelma Todd (Lorraine Lane); Josephine Dunn (Loris Lane); Thelda Kenvin (Betty Kent); Jeanne Morgan (Mae Oliver); Dorothy Nourse (Mary Arnold); Irving Hartley (Johnnie); Gregory Blackton (Frederick Maine); Robert Andrews (Duke Slade); Charles Brokaw (Gregory); Iris Gray (Sally Lee); Ralph Lewis (John Ward); Joseph Burke (Ward's Secretary); James Bradbury, Sr. (The

Professor); Harry Sweet (The Sheriff); William Black (Deputy Sheriff); Richard Dix; Adolphe Menjou; **Clara Bow**; Lois Wilson; Percy Marmont; Chester Conklin; Thomas Meighan; Lila Lee; Lewis Milestone; Malcolm St. Clair.

Synopsis: Clara Bow makes a cameo appearance as herself in this light collegiate comedy featuring a large ensemble of Paramount contract players. The story follows a group of lively young men and women competing for recognition at a prestigious training program for future studio talent. Bow's cameo adds star power to a film built to showcase the studio's rising generation. Her appearance is quick but unmistakably adds glamour and helps position the movie as a Paramount talent parade.

THE RUNAWAY (EXTANT IN FRAGMENTARY FORM) (Paramount, 1926) 6,218'

Director: William DeMille
Based on the story "The Flight to the Hills" by Charles Neville Buck
Screenplay: Albert Shilby LeVino
Camera: Charles Boyle.

Cast: Clara Bow (Cynthia Meade); Warner Baxter (Wade Murrell); William Powell (Jack Harrison); George Bancroft (Lesher Skidmore); Edythe Chapman (Mrs. Murrell).

Synopsis: Clara Bow stars as Cynthia Meade, a young woman forced to flee a troubled family situation and find refuge in the Kentucky mountains. There she becomes entangled with a rugged mountaineer and a morally ambiguous outsider, both of whom shape her struggle for safety and independence. Bow's performance was noted for its emotional intensity and physical boldness, contrasting the heroine's vulnerability with her fierce will to survive.

MANTRAP (EXTANT)
(Paramount, 1926) 6,077'

Producers: Hector Turnbull, B.P. Schulberg
Director: Victor Fleming
Based on the novel by Sinclair Lewis
Screenplay: Adelaide Heilbron
Titles: George Marion, Jr.
Camera: James Wong Howe

Cast: Ernest Torrence (Joe Aster); **Clara Bow (Alvena Easter)**; Percy Marmont (Ralph Prescott); Eugene Pallette (Woodbury); Tom Kennedy (Curly Evans); Josephine Crowell (Mrs. McGavvity); Charles Stevens (Jackfish); William Orlamond (McGarity); Miss Dupont (Mrs. Barker); Charlot Bird (Stenographer).

Synopsis: In one of her most acclaimed roles, Bow plays Alverna, an irrepressible small-town beauty who becomes the pivot of a romantic triangle between a mild-mannered lawyer and a gruff wilderness trapper. Alverna's desire for excitement and attention sets off a humorous but heartfelt conflict as the men chase her through forests, cabins, and backwoods communities. Bow's performance—playful, mischievous, and emotionally sharp—became a defining screen moment, capturing the modern flapper spirit with irresistible vitality. The film survives and remains one of her greatest works.

KID BOOTS (EXTANT)
(Paramount, 1926) 5,650'

Producer: B.P. Schulberg
Director: Frank Tuttle
Based on the play by William Anthony McGuire, Otto Harbach
Screenplay: Luther Reed, Tom Gibson

Titles: George Marion, Jr.
Camera: Victor Milner.

Cast: Eddie Cantor (Kid Boots); **Clara Bow (Jane Martin)**; Billie Dove (Polly Pendleton); Lawrence Gray (Tom Sterling); Natalie Kingston (Carmen Mendoza); Malcolm Waite (George Fitch); W.J. Worthington (Polly's Father); Harry von Meter (Polly's Lawyer); Fred Esmelton (Tom's Lawyer).

Synopsis: Clara Bow plays Jane Martin, a charming young woman vacationing at a luxurious resort where Eddie Cantor's bumbling golf caddy becomes embroiled in romantic trouble. Jane serves as the film's vivacious love interest, injecting glamour and spontaneity into the musical-comedy chaos surrounding her. Bow's breezy charm helps balance Cantor's broad comic antics, giving the story a romantic thread amid the slapstick.

"IT" (EXTANT)
(Paramount, 1927) 6,542'

Producers: Clarence Badger, Elinor Glyn
Associate producer: B.P. Schulberg
Director: Clarence Badger
Based on the novel by Elinor Glyn
Adaptation: Elinor Glyn
Screenplay: Hope Loring, Louis D. Lighton
Titles: George Marion, Jr.
Camera, H. Kinley Martin
Editor: E. Lloyd Sheldon.

Cast: Clara Bow (Betty Lou); Antonio Moreno (Cyrus Waltham); William Austin (Monty); Jacqueline Gadsdon (Jane Daly) (Adela Van Norman); Julia Swayne Gordon (Mrs. Van Norman); Priscilla Bonner (Molly); Eleanor Lawson, Rose Tapley (Welfare Workers) Elinor Glyn

(Herself); Lloyd Corrigan (Cabin Boy On Yacht); Gary Cooper (Reporter).

Synopsis: Bow's signature role casts her as Betty Lou Spence, a spirited shopgirl who pursues the handsome heir of a department-store empire with confidence, wit, and unshakable self-worth. As the embodiment of Elinor Glyn's concept of "It"—a magnetic quality beyond beauty or class—Betty Lou becomes the blueprint for the modern screen heroine. Bow's luminous performance turned her into an international icon and solidified the cultural meaning of the "It Girl." The film survives in good condition.

CHILDREN OF DIVORCE (EXTANT)
(Paramount, 1927) 6,871'

Associate producer: B. P. Schulberg
Producer: E. Lloyd Sheldon
Director: Frank Lloyd
Based on the novel by Owen Lloyd Johnson
Screenplay: Hope Loring, Louis D. Lighton
Camera: Victor Milner
Editor: E. Sheldon.

Cast: Clara Bow (Kitty Flanders); Esther Ralston (Jean Waddington); Gary Cooper (Ted Larrabee); Einar Hanson (Prince Ludovico de Sfax); Norman Trevor (Duke de Gondreville); Hedda Hopper (Katherine Flanders); Edward Martindel (Tom Larrabee); Julia Swayne Gordon (Princess de Sfax); Albert Gran (Mr. Seymour); Iris Stuart (Mousie); Margaret Campbell (Mother Superior); Percy Williams (Manning); Joyce Marie Coad (Little Kitty); Yvonne Pelletier (Little Jean); Don Marion (Little Ted).

Synopsis: Clara Bow plays Kitty Flanders, a young woman raised in a "divorce colony" who grows into adulthood traumatized by instability and desperate for security. Her impulsive marriage sets off a chain of emotional crises involving her childhood friend and his true love. Bow gives one of her strongest dramatic performances, portraying Kitty as both sympathetic and tragically self-destructive.

ROUGH HOUSE ROSIE (LOST FILM)
(Paramount, 1927) 5,952'

Associate producer: B.P. Schulberg
Director: Frank Strayer
Based on the story by Nunnally Johnson
Adaptation: Max Marcin
Screenplay, Louise Long, Ethel Doherty;
Assistant director, George Crook
Titles: George Marion, Jr.
Camera: James Murray, Hal Rosson.

Cast: Clara Bow (Rosie O'Reilly); Reed Howes (Joe Hennessey); Arthur Housman (Kid Farrell); Doris Hill (Ruth); Douglas Gilmore (Arthur Russell); John Miljan (Lew McKay); Henry Kolker (W. S. Davids).

Synopsis: Bow stars as Rosie O'Reilly, a tough, hardworking waitress whose resilience and charm draw the attention of a young man eager to prove himself. Rosie's refusal to be underestimated fuels a story of ambition, class aspiration, and small-town dreams. Contemporary reviews praised Bow's comedic verve and physicality. Although widely popular upon release, the film is now considered lost.

WINGS (EXTANT)
(Paramount, 1927) 12,682'

Associate producer: B.P. Schulberg
Producer: Lucien Hubbard
Director: William A. Wellman
Story: John Monks Saunders
Screenplay: Hope Loring, Louis D. Lighton
Music score: John S. Zamecnik
Assistant director: Richard Johnson
Aerial camera: E. Burton Steene, Sgt. Ward, Al Williams;
Titles: Julian Johnson
Engineering effects: Roy Pomeroy
Camera: Harry Perry
Editor, E. Lloyd Sheldon.

Cast: Clara Bow (Mary Preston); Charles "Buddy" Rogers (Jack Powell); Richard Arlen (David Armstrong); El Brendel (Herman Schwimpf); Jobyna Ralston (Sylvia Lewis); Richard Tucker (Air Commander); Gary Cooper (Cadet White), Gunboat Smith (Sergeant); Henry B. Walthall (Mr. Armstrong); Julia Swayne Gordon, (Mrs. Armstrong); Arlette Marchal (Celeste); George Irving (Mr. Powell); Hedda Hopper (Mrs. Powell); Nigel de Brulier (French Peasant); Roscoe Karns (Lt. Cameron); James Pierce (MP); Carl Von Haartman (German Officer).

Synopsis: In the first film ever to win the Academy Award for Best Picture, Bow plays Mary Preston, a small-town girl whose loyalty to two young aviators forms the emotional heart of the story. While the men train, fight, and drift apart amid the horrors of World War I, Mary endures her own trials as an ambulance driver in France. Bow's presence adds warmth and human stakes to the aerial spectacle, grounding the film's most intimate moments. A complete version survives.

HULA (EXTANT)
(Paramount, 1927) 5,862'

Associate producer: B.P. Schulberg
Director: Victor Fleming
Based on the novel by Armene Von Tempski
Adaptation: Doris Anderson
Screenplay: Ethel Doherty
Titles: George Marion, Jr.
Assistant director, Henry Hathaway
Camera, William Marshall
Editor; Eda Warren

Cast: Clara Bow ("Hula" Calhoun); Clive Brook (Anthony Haldane); Arlett Marchal (Mrs. Bane); Arnold Kent (Harry Dehan); Maude Truax (Margaret Haldane); Albert Gran (Old Bill Calhoun); Agostino Borgato (Uncle Edwin).

Synopsis: As Hula Calhoun, Bow delivers one of her boldest performances, playing a modern, uninhibited young woman living on a Hawaiian plantation. When she falls in love with a married English engineer, Hula pursues him with uninhibited confidence that pushes against social norms. Bow's portrayal blends flirtation, physical comedy, and emotional honesty, making Hula one of her most iconic flapper roles.

GET YOUR MAN (EXTANT IN FRAGMENTARY FORM)
(Paramount, 1927) 5,718'

Associate producer: B.P. Schulberg
Director: Dorothy Arzner
Based on the play Tu m'epouseras by Louis Verneuil
Continuity: Agnes Brand Leahy
Screenplay: Hope Loring

Titles: George Marion, Jr.
Camera, Alfred Gilks
Editor, Louis D. Lighton.

Cast: Clara Bow (Nancy Worthington); Charles "Buddy" Rogers (Robert de Bellecontre); Josef Swickard (Due de Bellecontre); Harvey Clark (Marquis de Villeneuve); Josephine Dunn (Simon de Villeneuve); Frances Raymond (Mrs. Worthington).

Synopsis: Bow stars as Nancy Worthington, an American tourist in Paris who sets her sights on a young nobleman already promised to another. With a blend of determination and humor, Nancy navigates chaperones, aristocratic obstacles, and a staged scandal to win her intended match. Full reels of the film survive, but some portions are missing, resulting in an incomplete restoration. Bow's performance remains charming and quick-witted in the surviving material.

RED HAIR (EXTANT IN FRAGMENTARY FORM)
(Paramount, 1928) 6,331'

Associate producer: B. P. Schulberg
Director: Clarence Badger
Based on the novel The Vicissitudes of Evangeline by Elinor Glyn
Adaptation: Percy Heath, Lloyd Corrigan
Assistant director: Archie Hill
Titles: George Marion, Jr.
Camera: Alfred Gilks
Editor: Doris Drought

Cast: Clara Bow ("Bubbles" McCoy); Lane Chandler (Robert Lennon); Lawrence Gran (Judge Rufus Lennon); Claude King (Thomas L. Burke); William Austin (Dr. Eusta, Gill); Jacqueline Gadson (Minnie Luther).

Synopsis: Bow plays Bubbles McCoy, an exuberant redheaded beauty whose flirtations, schemes, and romantic misadventures drive the film's lively narrative. Bubbles' fiery spirit and unapologetic confidence made the movie a showcase for Bow's comedic brilliance. Sadly, only a single reel featuring the Technicolor sequence survives, but it preserves a vivid glimpse of her performance.

LADIES OF THE MOB (LOST FILM)
(Paramount,1928) 6,792'

Director: William A. Wellman
Story: Ernest Booth
Adaptation: Oliver Garr, John Farrow
Titles: George Marion, Jr.
Camera: Henry Gerrard
Editor, Lloyd Sheldon

Cast: Clara Bow (Yvonne); Richard Arlen (Red); Helen Lynch (Marie); Mary Alden ("Soft Annie"); Carl Gerard (Joe); Bodil Rosing (Mother); Lorraine Rivero (Little Yvonne); James Pierce (The Officer).

Synopsis: In a darker, more dramatic turn, Bow portrays Yvonne, the daughter of a gangster who becomes entangled in a violent underworld she is desperate to escape. Her attempt to save the man she loves from the criminal life forms the tragic core of the story. Reviewers praised Bow for delivering a nuanced, emotionally powerful performance that stretched far beyond her comedic flapper persona. No known print survives.

THE FLEET'S IN (EXTANT IN FRAGMENTARY FORM)
(Paramount, 1928) 6,918'

Director: Malcolm St. Clair
Story-screenplay: Monte Brice, J. Walter Ruben

Titles: George Marion, Jr.
Camera, Harry Fischbeck
Editor; B. F. Zeidman.

Cast: Clara Bow (Trixie Deane); James Hall (Eddie Briggs); Jack Oakie (Searchlight Doyle); Eddie Dunn (Al Pearce); Jean Laverty (Betty); Dan Wolheim (Double Duty Duffy); Bodil Rosing (Mrs. Deane); Richard Carle (Judge Hartley); Joseph Gerard (Commandant).

Synopsis: Clara Bow plays Trixie Deane, a lively and flirtatious nightclub performer whose charm instantly entangles her with a pair of sailors on shore leave. Trixie's good humor and quick wit anchor a lighthearted romantic comedy built around misunderstandings, musical numbers, and the cheerful chaos of Navy life. Bow's performance gives the film its sparkle, portraying Trixie as both mischievous and sincere. The film survives only in an incomplete form, with missing footage.

THREE WEEKENDS (LOST FILM)
(Paramount, 1928) 5,962'

Director: Clarence Badger
Story: Elinor Glyn
Adaptation: John Farrow
Screenplay: Percy Heath, Louise Lang, Sam Mintz
Titles: Paul Perez, Herman Mankiewicz
Choreographer: Fanchon and Marco
Camera: Harold Rosson
Editor: Tay Malarkay.

Cast: Clara Bow (Gladys O'Brien); Neil Hamilton (James Gordon); Harrison Ford (Turner); Lucille Powers (Miss Witherspoon); Julia Swayne Gordon (Mrs. Witherspoon); Edythe Chapman (Ma O'Brien);

Guy Oliver (Pa Oliver); William Holden (Carter); Jack Raymond (Turner's Secretary).

Synopsis: Bow stars as Gladys O'Brien, a spirited chorus girl determined to seize any opportunity to escape the instability of showbusiness life. When she becomes involved with a wealthy young businessman, her plans collide with his sense of duty and family expectations. Bow gives the character a blend of ambition and vulnerability, portraying a woman trying to maintain her dignity while navigating a world of shifting promises. No known print is extant.

THE WILD PARTY (EXTANT)
(Paramount, 1929) 7,167'

Director: Dorothy Arzner
Story: Warner Fabian
Titles: E. Lloyd Sheldon, George Marion, Jr.
Dialogue: Sheldon, John V. A. Weaver
Costumes, Travis Banton
Song: Leo Robin and Richard Whiting
Camera: Victor Milner
Editor, Otho Lovering

Cast: Clara Bow (Stella Ames); Fredric March (Gil Gilmore); Shirley O'Hara (Helen Owens); Marceline Day (Faith Morgan); Joyce Compton (Eva Tutt); Adrienne Dore (Babs); Virginia Thomas (Tess); Kay Bryant (Maisie); Alice Adair (Thelma); Jean Lorraine (Ann); Renee Whitney (Janice); Amo Ingram (Jean); Jack Oakie (Al); Marguerite Cramer (Gwen); Phillips Holmes (Phil); Ben Hendricks, Jr. (Ed); Jack Luden (George); Jack Raymond (Baloam).

Synopsis: In her first talking picture, Bow portrays Stella Ames, a fun-loving college student whose carefree antics clash with the arrival of a stern young anthropology professor. Stella's exuberance stands at the center of a story about youthful rebellion, shifting social rules, and the tension between discipline and desire. Bow's natural energy helps smooth the transition to sound, and her slangy, modern delivery became one of the film's chief attractions.

THE SATURDAY NIGHT KID (EXTANT)
(Paramount, 1929) 63 M.

Director: A. Edward Sutherland
Based on the play Love 'Em and Leave 'Em by George Abbott,
    John V.A. Weaver
Screenplay: Lloyd Corrigan, Ethel Doherty
Dialogue: Corrigan, Edward Paramore, Jr.
Title: Joseph L. Mankiewicz
Camera: Harry Fishbeck
Editor: Jane Loring

Cast: Clara Bow (Mayme); James Hall (Bill); Jean Arthur (Janie); Charles Sellon (Lem Woodruff); Ethel Wales (Lily Woodruff); Edna May Oliver (Miss Streeter); Hyman Meyer (Ginsberg); Getty Bird (Riche); Frank Ross (Ken); Eddie Dunn (Jim); Leone Lane (Pearl); Jean Harlow (Hazel Carroll); Irving Bacon (McGonigle); Mary Gordon (Reducing Customer); Ernie Adams (Gambler); Alice Adair(Girl).

Synopsis: Bow plays Mayme, a hardworking department-store clerk at odds with her more irresponsible sister. When a theft accusation threatens their jobs and a romantic rivalry intensifies, Mayme must defend her integrity while holding her life together. Bow brings sharp emotional contrast to the role — warmth toward the characters she loves, and blazing frustration toward the ones who take advantage of her.

DANGEROUS CURVES (EXTANT)
(Paramount, 1929) 75 M.

Director: Lothar Mendes
Story: Lester Cohen
Screenplay: Donald Davis, Florence Ryerson
Dialogue: Viola Brothers Shore
Titles: George Marion, Jr.
Camera: Harry Fischbeck
Editor: Eda Warren

Cast: **Clara Bow (Pat Delaney)**; Richard Arlen (Larry Lee); Kay Francis (Zara Flynn); David Newell (Tony Barretti); Anders Randolf (G.P. Brock); May Boley (Ma Spinelli); T. Roy Barnes (Pa Spinelli); Joyce Compton (Jennie Silver); Charles D. Brown (Spider); Stuart Erwin (Rotarian); Oscar Smith (Bartender); Ethan Laidlaw (Roustabout); Russ Powell (Counterman), Jack Luden (Rotarian).

Synopsis: As Pat Delaney, a circus rider with aspirations of independence, Bow becomes entangled with a trapeze artist whose charm masks a self-destructive streak. Pat's loyalty, resilience, and yearning for self-respect shape the film's emotional arc as she struggles to balance romantic desire with her own future. Bow's performance — a mix of vulnerability and toughness — was widely praised, and the film remains one of her strongest sound-era features.

PARAMOUNT ON PARADE (EXTANT)
(Paramount, 1930) 102 M.

Producer: Albert A. Kaufman
Directors: Dorothy Arzner, Otto Brower, Edmund Goulding, Victor Heerman, Edwin H. Knopf, Rowland V. Lee, Ernst Lubitsch, Lothar Mendes, Victor Schertzinger, Edward Sutherland, Frank Tuttle

Choreographer: David Bennett
Production designer: John Wenger
Songs: Elsie Janis and Jack King; Sam Coslow; L. Wolfe Gilbert and Abel
Baer; Richard A. Whiting and Raymond Eagen; Richard A. Whiting and
Leo Robin; Ballard McDonald and Dave Dreyer; Mana-Zucca; Robin and
Ernesto De Curtis; David Franklin
Camera: Harry Fischbeck, Victor Milner
Editor: Merrill White

Cast: Richard Arlen, Jean Arthur, William Austin, George Bancroft, **Clara Bow**, Evelyn Brent, Mary Brian, Clive Brook, Virginia Bruce, Nancy Carroll, Ruth Chatterton, Maurice Chevalier, Gary Cooper, Leon Errol, Stuart Erwin, Kay Francis, Skeets Gallagher, Harry Green, Mitzi Green, James Hall, Phillips Holmes, Helen Kane, Dennis King, Abe Lyman & Band, Fredric March, Nino Martini, David Newell, Jack Oakie, Warner Oland, Zelma O'Neal, Eugene Pallette, Joan Peers, William Powell, Charles "Buddy" Rogers, Lillian Roth, Stanley Smith, Fay Wray, and: Iris Adrian, Mischa Auer, Cecil Cunningham, Robert Greig, Henry Fink, Jack Luden, Jack Pennick, Jackie Searle, Rolfe Sedan.

Synopsis: In this lavish all-star revue, Bow appears in a musical sketch that highlights her comic timing and exuberant personality. Her segment is one of many showcasing Paramount's major names in a series of musical and theatrical numbers. Although she does not anchor the narrative, Bow's presence adds sparkle to the film's flapper-era glamour. The film survives in multiple versions produced for different markets.

TRUE TO THE NAVY (EXTANT)
(Paramount, 1930) 71 M.

Director: Frank Tuttle
Story: Keene Thompson, Doris Anderson

Dialogue: Herman J. Mankiewicz
Songs: L. Wolfe Gilbert, Abel Baer
Camera: Victor Milner
Editor: Doris Drought

Cast: Clara Bow (Ruby Nolan); Fredric March (Bull's Eye McCoy); Harry Green (Solomon Birnberg); Rex Bell (Eddie); Eddie Fetherstone (Michael); Eddie Dunn (Albert); Ray Cooke (Peewee); Harry Sweet (Artie); Adele Windsor (Maizie); Sam Hardy (Brady); Jed Prouty (Dance-hall Manager); Charles Sullivan (Shore Patrol); Louise Beavers (The Maid); Frances Dee (Girl At Table); Maurice Black (Sharpie).

Synopsis: Bow stars as Ruby Nolan, a quick-witted soda-fountain girl whose romantic entanglement with a swaggering sailor leads to a blend of comedy, flirtation, and lighthearted rivalry. As Ruby, Bow shines with breezy confidence, embodying a working-class heroine who knows her own worth and refuses to be pushed around. Her banter and chemistry with Fredric March give the film much of its charm.

LOVE AMONG THE MILLIONAIRES (EXTANT)
(Paramount, 1930) 74 M.

Director: Frank Tuttle
Story: Keene Thompson
Screenplay: Grover Jones, William Conselman
Dialogue: Herman J. Mankiewicz
Songs: L. Wolfe Gilbert, Abel Baer
Camera: Allen Siegler

Cast: Clara Bow (Pepper Green); Stanley Smith (Jerry Hamilton); Skeets Gallagher (Boots McGee); Stuart Erwin (Clicker Watson); Mitzi Green (Penelope Green); Charles Sellon (Pop Green); Theodor von Eltz

(Jordan); Claude King (Mr. Hamilton); Barbara Bennett (Virginia Hamilton).

Synopsis: Bow plays Pepper Green, a waitress who falls for the son of a wealthy railroad magnate. Their romance becomes a test of class boundaries, public image, and personal ambition. Bow injects the story with lightness and sincerity, giving Pepper both comedic sparkle and emotional grounding. Musical numbers, mistaken identities, and rapid-fire dialogue keep the story moving briskly. The film survives.

HER WEDDING NIGHT (EXTANT)
(Paramount, 1930) 75 M.

Associate producer: E. Lloyd Sheldon
Director: Frank Tuttle
Based on the play by Avery Hopwood
Screenplay: Henry Myers
Camera: Harry Fischbeck
Editor: Doris Drought

Cast: Clara Bow (Norma Martin); Ralph Forbes (Larry Charters); Charlie Ruggles (Bertie Bird); Skeets Gallagher (Bob Talmadge); Geneva Mitchell (Marshall); Rosita Moreno (Lulu); Natalie Kingston (Eva); Wilson Bege (Smithers); Lillian Elliott (Mrs. Marshall).

Synopsis: As Norma Martin, a popular novelist accidentally mistaken for a notorious temptress, Bow becomes the center of a whirlwind of romantic misunderstandings and tabloid scandal. The film uses her comic gifts to full advantage, placing Norma in chaotic situations fueled by mistaken identity and eager suitors. Bow's playful timing and expressive reactions define the tone of the picture.

NO LIMIT (EXTANT)
(Paramount, 1931) 72 M.

Director: Frank Tuttle
Story: George Marion, Jr.
Screenplay: Viola Brothers Shore, Salisbury Field
Camera: Victor Milner
Editor: Tay Malarkey.

Cast: Clara Bow (Helen "Bunny" O'Day); Stuart Erwin (Ole Olsen); Norman Foster; (Douglas Thayer); Harry Green (Maxie Mindil); Dixie Lee (Dotty "Dodo" Potter);:' Mischa Auer (Romeo); Keene Duncan (Curley Andrews); G. Pat Collins (Charlie); Maurice Black (Happy); Frank Hagney (Battling Hannon); Paul Nicholson (Chief Q Detectives Armstrong); William B. Davidson (Wilkie, Building Superintendent); Lee Phelps (Ticket Taker); Robert Greig (Doorman); Allan Cavan (Board Member); Bill O'Brien (George The Butler); Perry Ivins (Butterfly Man); Sid Saylor (Reporter).

Synopsis: Bow stars as Helen "Bunny" O'Day, a spirited young woman whose involvement with a naïve elevator operator and a web of small-time crooks leads to a string of comedic escapades. Bunny navigates the trouble around her with boldness and charm, often outsmarting the men who underestimate her. Bow's lively delivery and rapid-fire energy are central to the film's appeal. The film survives.

KICK IN (EXTANT)
(Paramount, 1931) 75 M.

Director: Richard Wallace
Based on the play by Willard Mack
Screenplay: Barlett Cormack
Camera: Victor Milner.

Cast: Clara Bow (Molly Hewes); Regis Toomey (Chick Hewes); Wynne Gibson (Myrtle Sylvester); Juliette Compton (Piccadilly Bessie); Leslie Fenton (Charles); James Murray (Benny LaMarr); Donald Crisp (Harvey); Paul Hurst (Whip Fogarty); Wade Boteler (Diggs).

Synopsis: Bow plays Molly Hewes, the loyal wife of an ex-con determined to rebuild his life honestly despite pressure from corrupt figures and lingering suspicion from the law. Molly's devotion and moral strength guide the story, adding emotional depth to a tale of crime, redemption, and social prejudice. Bow delivers a restrained, heartfelt performance that contrasts with her comedy roles.

CALL HER SAVAGE (EXTANT)
(Fox, 1932) 92 M.

Associate producer: Sam E. Rork
Director: John Francis Dillon
Based on the novel by Tiffany Thayer
Screenplay: Edwin Burke
Art director: Max Parker
Assistant director: Jack Boland
Camera: Lee Garmes

Cast: Clara Bow (Nasa "Dynamite" Springer); Gilbert Roland (Moonglow); Monroe Owsley (Lawrence Crosby); Thelma Todd (Sunny De Lan); Estelle Taylor (Ruth Springer); Willard Robertson (Peter Springer); Weldon Heyburn (Ronasa); Arthur Hoyt (Attorney); Katherine Perry (Maid); John Elliott (Hank); Anthony Jowitt (Jay Randall); Hale Hamilton (Cyrus Randall); Mischa Auer (Agitator in Restaurant); Mary Gordon (Tenement Lady).

Synopsis: In one of her most powerful dramatic roles, Bow portrays Nasa "Dynamite" Springer, a rebellious young woman whose impulsive choices

and fierce temperament lead her through a series of turbulent relationships and shocking revelations about her heritage. The role allowed Bow
to display a wider emotional range than in many of her earlier films, shifting from sensuality to anger to vulnerability with striking force. The film
survives in excellent condition.

HOOP-LA (EXTANT)
(Fox, 1933) 85 M.

Director: Frank Lloyd
Based on the play The Barker by Kenyon Nicholson
Adaptation: Bradley King, J.M. March
Music score: Louis De Francesco
Camera: Ernest Palmer

Cast: Clara Bow (Lou); Preston Foster (Nifty); Richard Cromwell
(Chris); Herbert Mundin (Hap); James Gleason (Jerry); Minna Gombell
(Carrie); Florence Roberts (Ma Benson); Robert Imhof (Colonel Gowdy).

Synopsis: Bow's final film casts her as Lou, a seasoned carnival performer
who is persuaded to seduce an innocent young man to boost the show's
profits—only to find herself genuinely falling in love with him. Lou's in-
ternal conflict between her hardened exterior and her growing sincerity
gives Bow a poignant farewell role. Her performance blends warmth, sad-
ness, and resiliency, marking a fitting end to her screen career. The film
survives.

SELECTED BIBLIOGRAPHY

Basinger, Jeanine. *Silent Stars*. New York: Alfred A Knopf, 1999.

Bleitner, Thomas. *Women of the 1920s: Style, Glamour & the Avant-Garde*. New York: Abbeville Press Publishers, 2014.

Desjardins, Mary R. "An Appetite for Living: Gloria Swanson, Colleen Moore, and Clara Bow." In *Hollywood's Early Film Stars: An Anthology*, edited by Leslie Smith, 145-170. New York: Routledge, 2005.

Everson, William K. *American Silent Film*. New York: Oxford University Press, 1978.

Glyn, Elinor. *IT*. Las Vegas: Histria Perspectives, 2026.

Glyn, Elinor. *Romantic Adventure: Being the Autobiography of Elinor Glyn*. New York: E.P. Dutton & Co. Inc. Publishers, 1937.

Griffith, Richard, ed. *The Talkies: Articles and Illustrations from Photoplay Magazine, 1928-1940*. New York: Dover Publications, Inc., 1971.

Hallett, Hilary A. *Inventing the IT Girl: How Elinor Glyn Created the Modern Romance and Conquered Early Hollywood*. New York: Liveright Publishing Company, 2022.

Koszarski, Richard. *An Evening's Entertainment: The Age of the Silent Feature Picture, 1915-1928*. New York: Charles Scribner's Sons, 1990.

Mackrell, Judith. *Flappers: Six Women of a Dangerous Generation*. New York: Farrar, Straus and Giroux, 2021.

Morella, Joe, and Edward Z. Epstein. *The "It" Girl: The Incredible Story of Clara Bow*. New York: Delacorte Press, 1976.

Parish, James Robert. *The Paramount Pretties*. New York: Castle Books, 1972.

Photoplay Magazine. *Stars of the Photoplay*. Chicago: Photoplay Publishing Company, 1930.

Simon, Linda. *Lost Girls: The Invention of the Flapper*. London: Reaktion Books, 2017.

Stenn, David. *Clara Bow: Runnin' Wild*. New York: Doubleday, 1988.

Zierold, Norman. *Sex Goddesses of the Silent Screen*. Chicago: Henry Regnery Company, 1973.

Zeitz, Joshua. *Flapper: A Madcap Story of Sex, Style, Celebrity, and the Women Who Made America Modern*. New York: Crown Publishers, 2006.

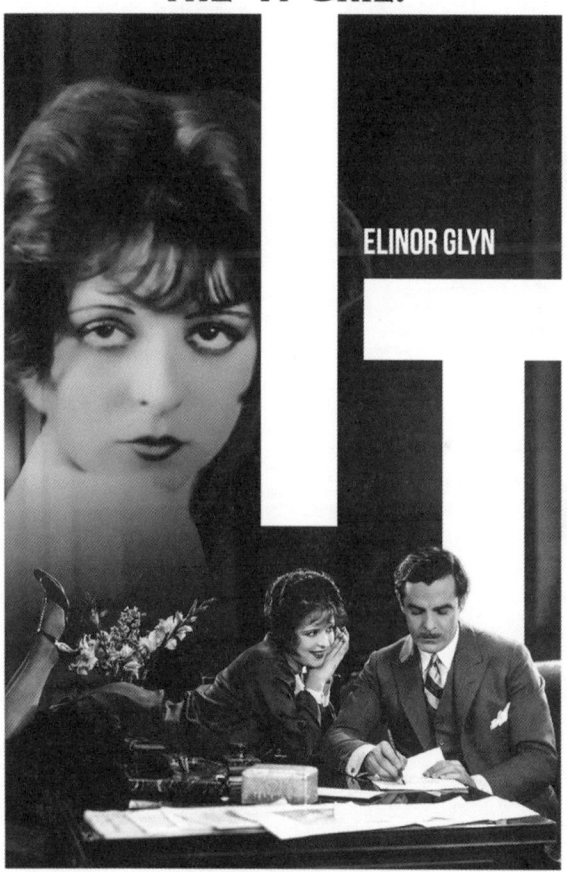